REVISE AQA GCSE
German

REVISION GUIDE

Series Consultant: Harry Smith   Author: Harriette Lanzer

THE REVISE AQA SERIES
Available in print or online

Online editions for all titles in the Revise AQA series are available Summer 2013.

Presented on our ActiveLearn platform, you can view the full book and customise it by adding notes, comments and weblinks.

Print editions

German Revision Guide	9781447941101
German Revision Workbook	9781447941149

Online editions

German Revision Guide	9781447941118
German Revision Workbook	9781447941156

Audio files
Audio files for the listening exercises in this book can be found at: www.pearsonschools.co.uk/mflrevisionaudio

This Revision Guide is designed to complement your classroom and home learning, and to help prepare you for the exam. It does not include all the content and skills needed for the complete course. It is designed to work in combination with Pearson's main AQA GCSE German 2009 Series.

To find out more visit:
www.pearsonschools.co.uk/aqagcseMFLrevision

ALWAYS LEARNING   **PEARSON**

Contents

Audio files

Audio files and transcripts for the listening exercises in this book can be found at: www.pearsonschools.co.uk/mflrevisionaudio

- -

A small bit of small print

AQA publishes Sample Assessment Material and the Specification on its website. This is the official content and this book should be used in conjunction with it. The questions in *Now try this* have been written to help you practise every topic in the book. Remember: the real exam questions may not look like this.

Target grades

Target grades are quoted in this book for some of the questions. Students targeting this grade should be aiming to get most of the marks available. Students targeting a higher grade should be aiming to get all of the marks available.

Birthdays

Make sure you can recognise months and dates. It is important that you do not mistake a month or a number.

Geburtstage

Januar Februar März April

Mai Juni Juli August

September Oktober November Dezember

Ich habe am vierten Mai Geburtstag.
My birthday is on 4th May.

Ich bin / wurde am dritten August 2001 geboren.
I was born on 3rd August 2001.

Dates

am

14 ⟶ Juli

am + date + month –
am vierzehnten Juli

im
⬇

im + month – im Juli

When you say a year, just use numbers. There is no word for 'in':
in 2010 – zweitausendzehn
in 1999 – neunzehnhundertneunundneunzig
and im Jahr 2012.

Worked example

 LISTENING 1 target F

Audio files

🎧 21 Audio files and transcripts can be found at: www.pearsonschools.co.uk/mflrevisionaudio

Listen to find out when Christian's birthday is.

A 27th May
B 16th June
C 26th June

Write the correct letter in the box. **C**

– Wann hast du Geburtstag, Christian?
– Ich habe am sechsundzwanzigsten Juni Geburtstag. Das ist am Sonntag!

Learning dates

Dates and numbers may come up in listening and reading exams so make sure you are confident with them.

• You're looking for two pieces of information – the date and the month.
• Only **one** of the dates here is correct, so make sure you get at least one piece of information to start narrowing your options.

Now try this

LISTENING 2 target C

Listen to three more people. Write the correct letters in the boxes.

A 29th March   **B** 30th October   **C** 18th May   **D** 17th May   **E** 29th October

1 ☐   **2** ☐   **3** ☐

Don't get confused between **Mai** (May) and **März** (March).
Listen twice if you like: once for the date, then once for the month.

Pets

To talk about your pets, make sure you are familiar with adjectives for colour, size and personality.

Haustiere

 der Goldfisch

 der Hund

 das Kaninchen

 die Katze

 die Maus

 das Meerschweinchen

 das Pferd

 der Vogel

 der Käfig

Separable verbs

Grammar page 96

Separable verbs break into two parts: main verb = second in the sentence, prefix = at the end.

ausführen – to take for a walk (animal)

Present	Ich führe den Hund aus.
Past	Ich habe den Hund ausgeführt.
Future	Ich werde den Hund ausführen.
Modals	Ich muss den Hund ausführen.

Other useful separable verbs to use:

auskommen mit	to get on with
einladen	to invite
(sich) vorstellen	to introduce (yourself)

Worked example

READING   *target B*

Listen to Markus talking about pets.
Which **two** statements express what he says?

A His parents are not strict.
B They have a goldfish at home.
C His brother would love to have a dog.
D Markus would love to have a dog.
E Markus wants to work with animals.

Write the correct letters in the boxes.

C   E

– Meine Eltern sind äußerst streng und zu Hause dürfen wir nicht einmal einen kleinen Goldfisch haben. Mein jüngerer Bruder wünscht sich jedes Jahr zum Geburtstag einen Hund – aber ohne Erfolg. Wenn ich älter bin, werde ich mit Tieren arbeiten und ich möchte auf dem Land wohnen, wo ich ein Pferd haben kann!

Listening tips

- Only write ONE letter in each answer box if that is what you are asked to do.
- Don't jump to conclusions as soon as you hear a word which matches an answer word.
- Listen to the WHOLE of the passage – the answers may not be revealed until the very end.

- You hear all of these options mentioned – you need to work out which are **true** and which are **not**.
- Make sure you are secure with the parts of the verb. It is Markus's brother who wants a dog (**wünscht**), not Markus (**wünsche**).
- Don't get tripped up by negatives. Watch out for crucial little words like **nicht** (not) and **kein** (not a).

Now try this

LISTENING 3   *target B*

Listen to Gabi talking about pets. Which **two** statements express what she says?

A She has a brown and white rabbit.
B She would love to have a dog.
C Her home is unsuitable.

D The park is far away.
E Her parents are allergic to dogs.

Write the correct letters in the boxes.   ☐   ☐

Physical description

In the speaking assessment you will need to describe yourself accurately if asked ...
but in the writing assessent you can describe your dream self!

Wie sehe ich aus?

Ich habe ... Haare.

blonde   graue

braune   schwarze

dunkle / helle	dark / light
glatte / lockige	straight / curly
kurze / lange	short / long
Ich habe (blaue) Augen.	I have (blue) eyes.
Er hat einen Bart / Schnurrbart.	He's got a beard / moustache.
Ich habe eine lange Nase.	I've got a long nose.

Sie trägt große Ohrringe.
She wears big earrings.

Ich trage eine Brille.
I wear glasses.

Comparing things
Grammar page 90

- For regular comparatives add -er to the adjective:

attraktiv	➡	attraktiver
dick(er)		fat(ter)
hässlich(er)		ugly (uglier)
hübsch(er)		pretty (prettier)
schlank(er)		slim(mer)
schön(er)		(more) beautiful

- The following are irregular:

alt	➡	älter	(old / older)
groß	➡	größer	(big / bigger)
gut	➡	besser	(good / better)
hoch	➡	höher	(high / higher)
jung	➡	jünger	(young / younger)

- Use als to compare:

Ich bin älter als du. I am older than you.

Worked example
READING *target C*

You read this news item in the local paper.

Der Verdächtige war ein Jugendlicher im Alter von siebzehn Jahren mit langen, dunkelbraunen Haaren und einem kleinen, braunen Bart. Er trug einen kleinen Ohrring im linken Ohr und hatte einen großen Hund dabei. Glücklicherweise hat die Polizei den Jungen erwischt, als er am folgenden Tag den Hund im Park ausgeführt hat.

Read the following sentence. Write **T** (True), **F** (False), or **?** (Not in the text) in the box.
The suspect was male. ☐ T

True, False, Not in the text

- Write the correct letter IN the box – don't write it above or below the box.
- If there is NO mention in the text of the item in the accompanying statement, then chances are the answer is ? (Not in the text).
- To count as F (False) the statement has to be CONTRADICTED in the text.

- Circle or underline key words to help you focus. In the first statement they are **der Verdächtige** (suspect) and **Bart** (beard).
- Even if you don't know the word **Verdächtige**, the fact that it is a **der** word tells you this is a male person. The use of **Er** later on confirms this.

Now try this
READING *target C*

Write **T** (True), **F** (False), or **?** (Not in the text) for these sentences about the above text.

(a) The suspect was 17 years old. ☐

(b) He wasn't wearing any jewellery. ☐

(c) His dog was not on a lead. ☐

(d) The suspect has been caught. ☐

Character description

To talk about character, you need to know the verb sein and lots of adjectives.

Charakterbeschreibung

Ich bin ...	I am ...
ehrlich	honest
ernst	serious
faul	lazy
fleißig	hard-working
frech	cheeky
(un)geduldig	(im)patient
gemein	mean / nasty
gut gelaunt	in a good mood
herrisch	domineering
(un)höflich	(im)polite
intelligent	intelligent
lebhaft	lively
lustig	funny
ruhig	quiet
sauer	cross
schüchtern	shy
traurig	sad
treu	loyal
unternehmungslustig	adventurous
witzig	funny / witty

The verb sein (to be)

ich	bin	I am
du	bist	you are
er / sie / es	ist	he / she / it is
wir	sind	we are
ihr	seid	you are
Sie / sie	sind	you / they are

Imperfect tense

ich war (I was)   sie waren (they were)

Eva ist intelligent, aber faul.

You may well need to distinguish between past and present characteristics:

Obwohl er heute frech ist, war er als Kind sehr schüchtern. Although he is cheeky today, he was very shy as a child.

Worked example

LISTENING 4 — target A

Listen to Erika's opinion of her new art teacher. How does she describe him?

A Relaxed   **B** Fun   **C** Serious

Write the correct letter in the box. ☐ C

– Ach, Mann. Ich freue mich jetzt gar nicht auf Kunst, weil der neue Lehrer schrecklich ist. Kunst sollte eigentlich Spaß machen und ein etwas lockeres Fach sein, aber Herr Jung ist so ernst, dass die wöchentliche Doppelstunde gar nicht lustig sein wird.

EXAM ALERT!

For this question you need to to be able to spot negatives. Many students understand vocabulary but overlook negatives, such as **nicht, nie, kein(e)** and so fail to understand properly.

Students have struggled with exam questions similar to this – **be prepared!**

ich freue mich nicht auf – I am not looking forward to
sollte Spaß machen – should be fun

Now try this

LISTENING 5 — target A

Listen to Daniel describing his best friend Thomas. What is Thomas like?

A Dominant	**B** Funny	**C** Shy	**D** Adventurous
E Boring	**F** Sometimes cross	**G** Honest	**H** Lazy

Write the **four** correct letters in the boxes.   ☐ ☐

Brothers and sisters

This page will help you to say lots about your brothers and sisters, even if you don't get on!

Geschwister

Geschwister (pl)   siblings

Zwillinge (pl)   twins

Meine Schwester geht mir auf die Nerven.
My sister gets on my nerves.

Bei uns gibt es immer Streit.
We are always having rows.

Ich kann meine Halbschwester nicht leiden.
I can't stand my half-sister.

Ich komme schlecht mit meinem Bruder aus.
I get on badly with my brother.

Ich verstehe mich gut mit meiner Schwester.
I get on well with my sister.

The verb haben (to have)

Present tense

ich	habe	I have
du	hast	you have
er / sie / es	hat	he / she / it has
wir	haben	we have
ihr	habt	you have
Sie / sie	haben	you / they have

Imperfect tense

ich hatte (I had)
wir hatten (we had)

Perfect tense

ich habe / er hat … gehabt
(I have / he has … had)

Vary the tense of **haben** to improve your sentences:

Als Kind habe ich mich oft mit meinem Bruder gestritten, aber jetzt haben wir ein gutes Verhältnis. As a child I often argued with my brother, but now we have a good relationship.

Worked example

target B

Read the text.

Ich verstehe mich gut mit meinen Schwestern, aber als Kind habe ich mich immer mit ihnen gestritten, weil sie so laut und gemein waren. Als ich dreizehn Jahre alt war, haben sich meine Eltern getrennt und ich musste mit meiner Mutter und meinen Schwestern umziehen. Wir mussten in das große Haus ihres Partners auf dem Land ziehen. Leider wohnte dort auch sein zwanzigjähriger Sohn, den ich nicht leiden konnte, weil er mich dauernd kritisierte.

Describe Anna's relationship with her sisters when they were young.

They argued all the time.

Reading tips

- Comprehension questions on a reading passage usually follow the order of the text.
- Read the whole question – here the last part of it 'when they were young' is crucial.

This question requires a knowledge of grammar. The question is not interested in Anna's current relationship with her sisters, but how they **used to** get on. So you must ignore references to the present ich verstehe … (I get on) and focus on habe mich … gestritten (argued).

Now try this

target B

Answer these questions on the above text.

(a) Why did Anna have to move house when she was 13?

(b) Describe Anna's relationship with her mother's partner's son.

Family

Include details of your family in any topic. It's crucial vocabulary to know and use.

Familie

Eltern (pl)	parents
Enkelkind (n)	grandchild
Neffe (m)	nephew
Nichte (f)	niece
Schwiegersohn (m)	son-in-law
Schwiegertochter (f)	daughter-in-law
Sohn (m)	son
Tochter (f)	daughter
adoptiert	adopted
alleinstehend	single
verliebt	in love
getrennt	separated
verheiratet	married
geschieden	divorced
ledig	unmarried

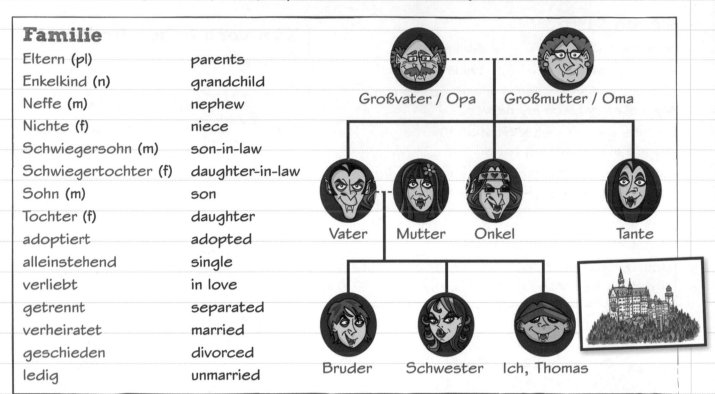

Großvater / Opa   Großmutter / Oma

Vater   Mutter   Onkel   Tante

Bruder   Schwester   Ich, Thomas

Worked example

SPEAKING

Was machst du am Wochenende mit deiner Familie?

AIMING HIGHER

In meiner Familie ist es Tradition, uns jedes Wochenende zusammen einen Fernsehfilm anzusehen. Wir machen dies bereits seit meiner Kindheit und nächstes Wochenende werden wir wieder zusammen auf dem Sofa sitzen und einen gemütlichen Familienabend genießen.

Aiming higher

Use different tenses to talk about your family:

✓ a special family event in the PAST

✓ a regular happening in the PRESENT, such as a visit to an elderly relative

✓ FUTURE family plans

✓ the sort of family you would rather have using the CONDITIONAL tense.

✓ Use seit + present tense to express how long you have been doing something.

Wir streiten uns schon seit vier Tagen.
We have been arguing for four days.

Now try this

SPEAKING

Use the advice above to help you include different tenses.

Answer the question about a family activity in 6–8 sentences.

• Was machst du mit deiner Familie?

Friends

Are friends the new family? Look at this page to help you give your opinion.

Freunde

Freunde finde ich sehr wichtig.
I find friends very important.

Mit guten Freunden ist man nie einsam.
You are never lonely with good friends.

Ich kenne meine Freundin seit der Grundschule.
I have known my girlfriend since primary school.

Unsere Freundschaft ist sehr stark.
Our friendship is very strong.

Mein idealer Typ wäre lustig und humorvoll.
My ideal guy would be funny with a good sense of humour.

Die ideale Freundin / Der ideale Freund sollte meiner Meinung nach lustig und sportlich sein.
The ideal friend, in my opinion, should be funny and sporty.

Wir kommen gut miteinander aus.
We get on well with each other.

Using sollen (should be)

Grammar page 98

sollen + infinitive

Ein guter Freund sollte treu sein.
A good friend should be loyal.

ich sollte	wir sollten
du solltest	ihr solltet
er / sie sollte	Sie / sie sollten

Ein guter Freund sollte …
A good (male) friend should …

Eine gute Freundin sollte …
A good (female) friend should …

… geduldig sein.
… be patient.

… immer Zeit für mich haben.
… always have time for me.

… nie schlechter Laune sein.
… never be in a bad mood.

… immer guter Laune sein.
… always be in a good mood.

Worked example

WRITING

Write about your best friend.

Mein bester Freund hat vier Beine und heißt Rex – das ist mein Hund! Er ist lustig und sehr lebhaft. Wir kommen gut miteinander aus. Mit ihm bin ich nie einsam.

AIMING HIGHER
Mein bester Freund hatte vier Beine und er war lustig und sehr lebhaft. Wir sind prima miteinander ausgekommen, aber leider ist er vor Kurzem gestorben, deshalb habe ich jetzt keinen besten Freund mehr. Ohne ihn finde ich das Leben einsam. Bald werde ich hoffentlich einen neuen Hund bekommen.

- Add something **unusual** or **quirky** to your work. This student decided to talk about his dog being his best friend, which is a refreshing approach.
- To improve his writing, this student could have adapted the text to include a tense other than the present.

This second student is writing at a higher level due to his secure use of a **variety of tenses**: imperfect, perfect, present and future.

Now try this

WRITING

Think of an 'unusual' best friend to write about in German, in about 100 words.

- Who is your best friend?
- What are his / her characteristics?
- Why do you get on with him / her?

Ich mag ihn / sie, weil + verb to the end.

Daily routine

You need to understand both the 12-hour and the 24-hour clock for the daily routine topic.

Mein Tagesablauf

Ich wache um sechs Uhr auf.	I wake up at 6 o'clock.
Ich stehe um zehn nach sechs auf.	I get up at ten past 6.
Zuerst bade ich.	First I have a bath.
Dann ziehe ich mich an.	Then I get dressed.
Ich frühstücke in der Küche.	I have breakfast in the kitchen.
Ich schminke mich.	I put on my make-up.
Ich putze mir die Zähne.	I brush my teeth.
Um zehn vor acht ...	At ten to 8 ...
verlasse ich das Haus.	I leave home.
fahre ich mit dem Bus in die Schule.	I go to school by bus.

Um vier Uhr komme ich nach Hause zurück.
At 4 o'clock I return home.

Um zehn Uhr gehe ich schlafen.
I go to sleep at 10 o'clock.

um – at
gegen – around

12-hour clock

 zwei Uhr

 fünf nach zwei

 Viertel nach zwei

 halb drei

Be careful! **Halb drei** is half-past two (literally, half **to** three)

 Viertel vor drei

 zehn vor drei

Now try this

Speak for **one** minute about your daily routine once you come back from school.
- Was machst du nach der Schule?

Include a description of a specific incident in the **past** to help raise your level.

Breakfast

Food may come up as a topic. Make sure you can say what you eat and when.

Das Frühstück

die Bratwurst
das Müsli
das Obst
eine Tasse Kaffee
das Toastbrot
das Spiegelei
ein Glas Milch
der Joghurt
der Fruchtsaft

Here are some other breakfast words you may need to know:

Brötchen (n) / Brot (n)	bread roll / bread	Marmelade (f)	jam
Ei (n)	egg	Honig (m)	honey
Rührei (n)	scrambled egg	Haferbrei (m)	porridge

Worked example WRITING

Write about your breakfast on a Sunday.

Am Sonntag bleibe ich bis dreizehn Uhr im Bett, weil ich am Wochenende nicht für die Schule aufstehen muss! Am liebsten esse ich ein Spiegelei mit Toastbrot und Ketchup und trinke ich dazu eine große Tasse Kaffee.

AIMING HIGHER Nachdem ich gefrühstückt habe, setze ich mich vor den Fernseher und sehe mir die vielen Sendungen an, die ich während der Woche nicht gesehen habe. Das ist meine Lieblingsaktivität, aber leider muss ich danach Hausaufgaben machen. Das finde ich nicht so gut!

Days of the week

Use **am** to describe days of the week:
am Montag - on Monday

Sonntag	Montag	Dienstag	Mittwoch	Donnerstag	Freitag	Samstag
	1	2	3	4	5	6
7	8	9	10	11	12	13

To aim higher, add a relative pronoun with the past tense:

... **die ich während der Woche nicht gesehen habe**

... that I didn't watch during the week.

Now try this WRITING

Write about 100 words answering the following questions:

1 Was isst du normalerweise zum Frühstück?
2 Was hast du letzten Sonntag zum Frühstück gegessen und getrunken?
3 Wie wäre dein ideales Frühstück?

- Make your answer more interesting by adding an **inversion**.
- Always give **reasons** using **weil** (because) plus a verb.
- Add simple adjectives like **große** to show you can make your adjectives **agree** with your nouns.

Eating at home

Make sure you know lots of food and drink vocabulary to enable you to talk about eating at home.

Zu Hause essen

Ich habe Hunger / Durst.
I am hungry / thirsty.

Ich bin satt.
I am full.

Mittagessen (n)
lunch

Abendessen (n)
evening meal

Eis (n)
ice-cream

Fisch (m)
fish

Gemüse (npl)
vegetables

Obst (n)
fruit

Hähnchen (n)
chicken

Kartoffel (f)	potato
Nudeln (fpl)	pasta
Reis (m)	rice
Salat (m)	salad
Schokolade (f)	chocolate
Schweinefleisch (m)	pork
braten	to roast, fry
vorbereiten	to prepare
fettig	greasy, fatty
fettarm	low-fat
köstlich / lecker	delicious
roh	raw
süß	sweet
scharf / würzig	spicy / hot

Opinions

Use schmecken to say if you do or don't like an item of food (literally 'It tastes to me good').

schmecken is followed by the dative case, so it needs mir.

Die Suppe (singular noun = one of it)

schmeckt mir gut.
The soup tastes good.

Die Himbeeren schmecken mir nicht.
I don't like the raspberries.

Schmeckt dir das Hähnchen?
Do you like the chicken?

Worked example

READING · target C

Read the healthy eating advice.

Mittagessen
Wir empfehlen gebackenen Fisch oder gegrilltes Hähnchen mit Reis oder Nudeln und Gemüse. Essen Sie doch mal Desserts mit frischem Obst und Vanilleeis oder Joghurt.

Abendessen
Essen Sie am Abend nur ein leichtes Essen, wie Karotten, Gurke und Spargel mit Dipp, Salat oder Suppe. Trinken Sie dazu Wasser oder einen gesunden Fruchtsaft.

Is pasta recommended for lunch **L**, supper **S** or both **L + S**?
Write the correct letter in the box.
Pasta ☐ L

- Identify the German term for the food item first. Here, you are looking for **Nudeln**.

- Sometimes the word will not be exactly as you expect it – for example 'vegetables' could be given as individual items, **Kartoffeln, Bohnen**, rather than the collective term, **Gemüse**.

- Check the text headings **L** for **Mittagessen** (lunch), **S** for **Abendessen** (supper) and **L + S** (both) to make sure you note the correct letter(s).

Now try this

READING · target C

Look at the text above. Are these items recommended for lunch **L**, supper **S** or both **L + S**?

(a) Chicken ☐   **(b)** Vegetables ☐   **(c)** Soup ☐

Eating in a café

Many of these food words look very similar to English, so you should recognise them in a reading or listening passage.

Im Café

Ich habe ... bestellt. I ordered ...

Fruchtsaft (m) — Limonade (f)

Milch (f)

Mineralwasser (n)

Ich hätte gern einmal ...	I would like a portion of ...
Hamburger (m)	hamburger
Omelett (n)	omelette
Pommes (frites) (pl)	chips
Schaschlik (m)	kebab
Bratwurst (f) mit Senf	fried sausage with mustard

Saying 'how many'

- Use number + mal (all one word, lower case) when ordering food portions:

  Ich möchte bitte einmal Pommes frites mit Ketchup.

  I'd like one portion of chips with ketchup, please.

- Use the same construction when talking about how often you do something:

  Letztes Jahr bin ich dreimal pro Woche ins Café gegangen.
  Last year I went to the café three times a week.

Guten Appetit!

There are many sausage varieties in Germany, so make sure you are familiar with these!

Bockwurst – bockwurst

Bratwurst – fried sausage

Currywurst – sausage with curry sauce

mit – with
ohne – without
Essig – vinegar

Ketchup – ketchup
Mayonnaise – mayonnaise
Senf – mustard

Worked example LISTENING 6 target G

What does Jonas order at the snack bar?

A  B C

Write the correct letter in the box. [C]

– Was möchtest du, Jonas?
– Einmal Pommes frites, bitte.

EXAM ALERT!

The topic of food is very familiar and this sort of task offers a good opportunity for you to do well – but some students made mistakes because they did not know this basic vocabulary.

Students have struggled with exam questions similar to this – **be prepared!**

Now try this LISTENING 7 target G

Now listen and note what Llayda, Lukas and Benjamin order. Write the correct letter.

1 Llayda ☐ A   B   C

2 Lukas ☐ A   B   C

3 Benjamin ☐ A   B C

Eating in a restaurant

Always try to include adjectives when talking about restauarants and impress with correct endings.

Im Restaurant

Auswahl (f)	selection / choice
Speisekarte (f)	menu
Speisesaal (m)	dining room
Spezialität (f)	speciality
Tagesgericht (n)	dish of the day
Hauptgericht (n)	main course

die Speisekarte

das Glas

die Gabel

die Schokoladentorte

die Serviette

der Teller
das Messer
der Löffel

Adjective endings (der, die, das)

 Grammar page 89

Masculine nouns

nom	acc	dat	
der	den	dem	Mann
gute	guten	guten	Hund

Feminine nouns

nom / acc	dat	
die	der	Frau
gute	guten	Katze

Neuter nouns

nom / acc	dat	
das	dem	Kind
gute	guten	Getränk

Plural nouns

nom / acc	dat	
die	den	Freunde(n)
guten	guten	Servietten

Worked example LISTENING 8   target A

Mohammed is talking about a restaurant with a new manager.

Note something which has …

(a) not changed.

The food is excellent.

(b) changed.

Prices have gone up by 10%.

– Welches Restaurant hast du besucht?

– Das neue, das einer hässlichen Baustelle gegenüber ist. Ich gehe oft dahin, aber jetzt gibt es einen neuen Manager und obwohl das Essen noch ausgezeichnet ist, sind die Preise alle zehn Prozent teurer als früher. Das finde ich mies.

EXAM ALERT!

- For the higher grades, you need to be able to answer each question with the precise detail you hear. That means you must read the question **very** carefully so you don't write down something which is irrelevant.
- Picking out key words is not enough here, as you have to understand the structure of the sentence after **obwohl** (although), which contains the comparative form of **teuer – teurer** (more expensive). Make sure you learn plenty of adjectives along with their comparative forms.

Students have struggled with exam questions similar to this – **be prepared!**

Now try this LISTENING 9   target A

Now listen to Sandra and Felix and answer the questions.

1 (a) What did Sandra feel about the bill?

  (b) Why is Sandra keen to earn some money?

2 (a) What was the problem when Felix went to order a pizza?

  (b) Why did Felix not order a pizza?

Healthy eating

Learn some of the phrases on this page so that you can talk confidently about healthy eating.

Gesundheit

Normalerweise esse ich gesund.
I normally eat healthily.

Ich habe zugenommen.
I have put on weight.

Ich möchte ein Kilo abnehmen.
I would like to lose a kilo.

Ich esse zu viele Bonbons / Süßigkeiten.
I eat too many sweets.

Morgen fange ich eine Diät an.
I am going on a diet tomorrow.

Ich esse wenig Fett oder Salz.
I don't eat much salt or fat.

dünn / schlank	thin / slim
magersüchtig	anorexic
übergewichtig	overweight
vegetarisch	vegetarian

Three key tenses

Past tense
- form of haben / sein + past participles
- watch out for imperfects war (was), hatte (had), es gab (there was / were)
- and pluperfect hatte gemacht (had done), war gefahren (had gone).

Present tense
- ends in -e for ich form and -t for er / sie form
- mind the irregulars: liest (reads), fährt (goes), isst (eats).

Future tense
- form of werden (werde, wird) + infinitive
- watch out for future conditionals würde (would) + infinitive and wäre (would be), möchte (would like) + infinitive.

Worked example

- **als** (when) usually indicates past tense.
- **jetzt** (now) indicates present tense.

Frannie is talking about her eating habits.

Als ich jünger war, habe ich oft fettige Mahlzeiten und viel Fastfood gegessen, aber das finde ich jetzt zu ungesund. Ich bin sportlich und will ein gesundes Leben führen, weil ich das sehr wichtig finde. Seit einem Jahr bin ich Vegetarierin und vegetarisches Essen gefällt mir gut, weil es sehr gesund ist. Ich habe keine Lust, wieder Fleisch zu essen, aber meine Mutter verlangt, dass ich zweimal pro Woche Fisch zu Mittag esse.

Which sentence is correct?

A Frannie has always had a healthy diet.
B Frannie sometimes eats fish.
C Frannie used to be a vegetarian.

Write the correct letter in the box. ☐ B

EXAM ALERT!

Some students tend to muddle the past and present tense in questions like this, and so struggle to identify the correct sentence. You need to revise tenses carefully in order to recognise them in reading and listening passages.

Students have struggled with exam questions similar to this – **be prepared!**

Now try this

Read the above text again. Which two sentences are correct?

A Frannie doesn't find diet important.
C Frannie's mother cares about what Frannie eats.
B Frannie is keen to have a healthy diet.
D Frannie is sometimes tempted to eat meat.

Write the letters in the boxes. ☐ ☐

Health issues

Naming a body part and adding -schmerzen (pain) is an easy way to express where it hurts!

Krankheiten

Es geht mir gut / schlecht.	I'm well / ill.
Ich bin / fühle mich krank.	I am / feel ill.
Mir ist übel.	I feel sick.
Schmerz (m)	pain
erste Hilfe (f)	first aid
hungrig / durstig	hungry / thirsty
tot	dead
gebrochen	broken
atmen	to breathe
sich entspannen	to relax
sich erbrechen	to vomit
Ich habe ...	I've got ...

Magenschmerzen (pl)   Halsschmerzen (pl)
Bauchschmerzen (pl)

Kopfschmerzen (pl)   Rückenschmerzen (pl)

Saying something hurts

Mein(e) ... tut weh. My .... hurts.

Use tut (one thing) or tun (more than one thing) + weh.

↓

Mein Fuß tut weh. My foot hurts.

↓

Meine Füße tun weh. My feet hurt.

Past pain to talk about? Easy:

Meine Hand tat weh. My hand hurt.

↓

Meine Arme taten weh. My arms hurt.

Bein (n)	leg
Finger (m)	finger
Knie (n)	knee
Schulter (f)	shoulder

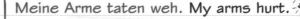

Worked example

WRITING

Write about an accident.

AIMING HIGHER
Letztes Jahr konnte ich nicht in den Skiurlaub fahren, weil ich stattdessen mit gebrochenem Bein zu Hause bleiben musste. Es war ziemlich schade, denn drei Tage vor dem Urlaub bin ich beim Eishockeytraining voll ausgerutscht. Ich wusste sofort, dass es schlimm war, weil ich nicht wieder aufstehen konnte. Ich wurde ins Krankenhaus gebracht, wo ich einen Gips bekam. Mensch, war das ein Pech!

Gips (m) – plaster cast

Aiming higher

Challenge yourself to include the following to achieve your best possible written work.

1. Weil and dass clauses
2. Dative prepositional phrases: mit gebrochenem Bein (with a broken leg), beim Eishockeytraining (at ice hockey training)
3. Correct word order: TIME, MANNER, PLACE
4. Modal verbs in the imperfect: konnte, musste, wusste
5. Idioms: es war schade (it was a shame / pity), Pech (bad luck)

Now try this

WRITING

Imagine you had an accident which meant you could not do something you really wanted to. Write about 200 words.

- Describe the accident.
- What did it stop you doing?

- Did anything positive come out of the accident? Describe it.

Look back at the bullet points above and include as many elements as possible in your writing.

Health problems

Alcohol, drugs and smoking are the focus here. This vocabulary is mainly for Higher level students who want to cover these issues in the assessments.

Gesundheitsprobleme

Alkohol (m)	alcohol
alkoholfrei	alcohol-free
alkoholisch	alcoholic
betrunken	drunk
Entziehungskur (f)	rehab
Gewohnheit (f)	habit
Sucht (f)	addiction
rauchen	to smoke
Raucher (m)	smoker
Rauschgift (n)	drugs
Tabak (m)	tobacco
Tablette (f)	tablet, pill
Zigarette (f)	cigarette
abhängig	dependent
aufhören	to stop
bewusstlos	unconscious
probieren	to try
schädlich	harmful
spritzen	to inject

Present tense irregulars

Grammar page 95

aufgeben – to give up

ich	gebe ... auf
du	gibst
er / sie / es	gibt
wir	geben
ihr	gebt
Sie/sie	geben

vowel change

sterben – to die

ich	sterbe
du	stirbst
er / sie / es	stirbt

nehmen – to take

ich	nehme
du	nimmst
er / sie / es	nimmt

essen – to eat

ich	esse
du	isst
er / sie / es	isst

Learning vocabulary

Look at the 'word family' for Alkohol.

Alkohol (m) alcohol

- alkoholfrei — alcohol-free
- alkoholisch — alcoholic
- alkoholarm — low in alcohol
- alkoholsüchtig — addicted to alcohol
- Alkoholiker/in (m/f) — an alcoholic

Worked example

READING · target A

Lukas has written about his health. Does this sentence relate to Lukas **L**, Susanne **S** or both **L + S**?

I can't stop smoking. ☐ L

The start of the text is all in the 'I' form, **ich**, and you already know Lukas is the writer, so the statement refers to himself. You have to read on to find out if it also refers to Susanne or not.

Ich rauche seit fünf Jahren. Es ist zu einer schlimmen Gewohnheit geworden und ich habe oft versucht, aufzuhören, aber ich habe es nie geschafft. Sobald jemand mir eine Zigarette gibt .... fange ich wieder an, obwohl ich weiß, dass Zigaretten sehr schädlich sind. Neulich habe ich bemerkt, dass ich beim Fußballspielen nicht so schnell laufen kann, weil ich an Atembeschwerden leide. Meine Freundin Susanne raucht nicht und würde auch nie damit anfangen, aber sie ist immer krank und gestern hat sie den ganzen Tag lang Kopfschmerzen gehabt. Am Abend konnte sie nicht schlafen, weil sie immer wieder gehustet hat. Sie sagt, es ist wegen meiner Zigaretten, aber ich glaube, dass sie hustet, weil sie nicht fit ist und keinen Sport treibt.

Now try this

READING · target A

Do these sentences relate to Lukas **L**, Susanne **S** or both **L + S**?

(a) I have health issues. ☐

(b) Cigarettes have a negative effect on my sports performance. ☐

(c) I think cigarettes damage your health. ☐

(d) I suffer from a cough. ☐

Future relationship plans

Married? Single? Be prepared to say something in German about your relationship plans!

Zukunftspläne

Braut (f)	bride
Bräutigam (m)	groom
Erwachsene (m/f)	adult
Frau (f)	wife / woman
Mann (m)	husband / man
Freund / Freundin (m/f)	boy / girlfriend
Freundschaft (f)	friendship
Gefühl (n)	feeling
Trauring (m)	wedding ring
Verlobungsring (m)	engagement ring
heiraten	to marry
sich scheiden lassen	to get divorced
sich trennen	to separate
sich verloben	to get engaged
warten	to wait
allein / ledig	alone / single
verlobt	engaged

Expressing opinions

Use a range of opinion / reaction expressions in your speaking assessment.

Das ist traurig.	That's sad.
Das ist besser.	That's better.
Das geht.	That's OK.
Das finde ich unfair.	I think that's unfair.
Das ist schrecklich!	That's dreadful!
Ich habe Angst davor.	I'm afraid of that.

Meiner Meinung nach ...
In my opinion ...

Ich glaube / denke, dass ... (+ verb to the end)
I believe / think that ...

Ich bin (nicht) damit einverstanden.
I (don't) agree with that.

> Ich glaube, dass ich in Zukunft heiraten werde.

Worked example

Willst du heiraten?

Ich möchte einen reichen Freund finden. Ich möchte ihn heiraten und Kinder haben. Ich suche schon den Trauring aus!

This is a solid answer. The student uses the present and the conditional **ich möchte** + verb to the end. She also gets her accusative gender correct, **den Trauring**.

AIMING HIGHER

Ich will nie heiraten. Vor drei Jahren haben sich meine Eltern scheiden lassen, weil mein Vater sich in eine Frau auf der Arbeit verliebt hat. Meiner Meinung nach bringt eine Hochzeit nur Stress und Streit. Da ich keine Kinder haben möchte, wäre das für mich eine totale Zeitverschwendung. Das ledige Leben ist viel einfacher und man hat weniger Probleme damit.

- To aim higher, this student uses more complex structures: **weil mein Vater sich in eine Frau auf der Arbeit verliebt hat** (because my father fell in love with a woman at work).
- She also uses conditional forms **wäre** (would be) and **möchte** + infinitive (would like to).
- The candidate has also stretched herself to include interesting vocabulary such as **Zeitverschwendung** (waste of time).

Now try this

Prepare answers to these questions giving details of your plans. Speak for about 30 seconds on each.

- Möchtest du eines Tages heiraten? Warum (nicht)?
- Möchtest du Kinder haben? Warum (nicht)?

Social issues

Use this page to help you discuss social issues in German.

Probleme in der Gesellschaft

arbeitslos	unemployed
arm / reich	poor / rich
multikulturell	multicultural
obdachlos	homeless
bedürftig	needy
heutzutage	nowadays
Abstinenz (f)	abstinence
AIDS	AIDS
HIV positiv	HIV positive
Armut (f)	poverty
Blödsinn (m)	nonsense
Diskriminierung (f)	discrimination
Freiwillige (m/f)	volunteer
Gewalt (f)	violence
Gleichheit (f)	equality
Grund (m)	reason / cause
Rassismus (m)	racism

Qualifiers

Qualifier + adjective = 😊

gar nicht	not at all
nicht	not
ein bisschen	a bit
ganz	quite
ziemlich	quite
meistens	mostly
sehr	very
besonders	especially

In den großen Städten ist die Armut besonders schrecklich.

Poverty is especially bad in big cities.

Worked example

Read the text and choose the correct title.

Meiner Meinung nach sollten wir alle zusammen gegen das Problem kämpfen. Wir sollten an die Politiker schreiben und verlangen, dass sie uns Gleichheit bei der Arbeit garantieren. Gemeinsam sind wir stark!

Write the correct letter in the box. ☐ B

A Fighting for better pay
B Asking the government for help
C Helping employers

EXAM ALERT!

- Some students jump to conclusions too early in a task (in this example on the word **kämpfen** – to fight) and note their answers before they have read the rest of the text.
- Make sure you learn lots of verbs, not just nouns and read the text **very** carefully.
- Read all the multiple choice options and all the text **before** you make your choice.

Students have struggled with exam questions similar to this – **be prepared!**

Now try this

Which title matches the story? Write the correct letter in the box.

Wenn ich Bundeskanzler wäre, würde ich gegen Rassismus aller Art kämpfen. Ich würde es weder in der Schule noch am Arbeitsplatz vertragen. Unsere Gesellschaft muss mir dabei helfen, sodass wir eine bessere Welt für die nächste Generation schaffen können.

A Racism must be eradicated
B Discrimination at school is common
C The next generation must fight their own battles ☐

Social problems

You may meet more complex vocabulary in the Higher paper, so learn it well if you're aiming high!

Probleme in der Gesellschaft

Einwanderer (m)	immigrant
Hautfarbe (f)	skin colour
Freiwillige (m/f)	volunteer
Gastfreundschaft (f)	hospitality
Kriminalität (f)	criminality
Not (f)	distress
Opfer (n)	victim
Rasse (f)	race
Rassenprobleme (pl)	race problems
rassistisch	racist
Rentner (m)	pensioner
Vandalismus (m)	vandalism
Verbrechen (n)	crime
Wohltätigkeit (f)	charity
beitragen zu	to contribute to
benachteiligen	to disadvantage
sich schämen	to be ashamed
sorgen für	to care for
spenden	to donate
unterstützen	to support

Comparisons

> Grammar page 90

Watch out for comparatives and superlatives in listening and reading passages.

Das Problem ist … The problem is …	… schlimm. … terrible.
	… schlimmer als letztes Jahr. … more terrible than last year.
	… am schlimmsten. … most terrible.
	… eines der schlimmsten Probleme in Deutschland. … one of the most terrible problems in Germany.

Zeig Rassismus die rote Karte

Worked example

 LISTENING 10   target B

Rudi is talking about the work he does with a local organisation. What does he say about the incident at his block of flats?

A He knew the boy who was stabbed.
B His friend had a knife.
C He wasn't affected by the incident.
Write the correct letter in the box.   A

– Ja, vor drei Jahren wurde mein bester Freund Opfer eines rassistischen Angriffs in meiner Gegend. Ein Junge hat ihn im Korridor des Wohnblocks mit einem Messer verletzt. Ich habe mich damals sehr geschämt, …

Listening tips

- Use any English words in the question to help you understand. Here, you are going to hear something about an 'incident at his block of flats'.

- You won't necessarily hear exact translations of the choices on the paper. Listen for words from the same family, such as hoffen (to hope) and hoffnungsvoll (hopeful).

- Don't jump to conclusions – you need to listen to all of the passage to check you have made the correct choice.

Now try this

 LISTENING 10   target B

Listen to the rest of the passage and write the correct letter in the box.

How does Rudi feel about the problem now?   ☐

A He doesn't think the race problems can be solved.
B He thinks his group can solve all the problems.
C He thinks his group may have a solution.

General hobbies

Make sure you have plenty of ideas on leisure time activities to talk about.

Hobbys

Ich sehe gern fern.

Ich spiele gern am Computer.

Ich höre gern Musik.

Ich koche gern.

Ich lese gern.

Ich spiele gern Schach.

Ich schicke gern SMS.

Ich gehe gern kegeln.

Present tense (regular)

Grammar page 95

I make / I am making / I do make

machen – **to do / to make**

ich	mache
du	machst
er / sie / es	macht
wir	machen
ihr	macht
Sie / sie	machen

infinitive

Ich mache Fitnesstraining.
I do training

Ich gehe gern aus.
I like going out.

Worked example

 LISTENING 12   target E

What does Belinda enjoy doing in her free time?

A Shopping

B Making cakes

C Going out

Write the correct letter in the box. ☐ B

– In meiner Freizeit bin ich meistens in der Küche zu finden, weil ich sehr gern backe.

- You are not necessarily going to hear the exact phrase you are familiar with, but you will hear enough to lead you to the words you know.
- Belinda says she is mostly **in der Küche. Küche** = kitchen, so select the answer option which is related to this.
- There is only one suitable answer here, which is B Making cakes. Nothing else is vaguely related to 'kitchen' or 'baking'.

Now try this

LISTENING 13   target E

Listen to the rest of the recording and write the correct letter in the box for these people's hobbies.

1 A Computer	**B** Television	**C** Cycling	☐
2 A Music	**B** Walking	**C** Bowling	☐
3 A Sport	**B** Cinema	**C** Reading	☐

Don't miss the negative **nicht** for the third speaker.

Sport

You may want to refer to sports when talking about various topics. Make sure the main VERB always comes in SECOND position in a sentence.

Sportarten

Ich ...

angle

jogge

reite

fahre Rad

fahre Skateboard

gehe schwimmen

mache Gymnastik

mache Leichtathletik

laufe Rollschuh

spiele Fußball

spiele Tischtennis

treibe Sport

Verb in second place

Grammar page 92

❶ Ich ❷ spiele ❸ Handball.

❶ Im Winter ❷ spiele ❸ ich Handball.

In the perfect tense, the part of haben or sein goes in second place.

❶ Im Winter ❷ habe ❸ ich Handball ❹ gespielt.

Im Sommer spiele ich Tennis.

Worked example 🗣 SPEAKING

Welche Sportarten treibst du?

AIMING HIGHER
Ich bin sehr aktiv und treibe dreimal in der Woche Sport. Letztes Jahr war es ganz anders, weil ich mir das Bein gebrochen hatte und vier Monate lang keinen Sport treiben konnte. Das war eine Katastrophe für mich und ich musste dauernd am Computer spielen – was ich langweilig fand. Mein Traum ist es, eines Tages Profifußballspieler zu werden und ich würde am allerliebsten für Chelsea spielen.

Aiming higher

Including three tenses in your work is as easy as ... 1, 2, 3, if you can say which sports you:

❶ DO now
❷ DID previously
❸ WOULD LIKE or WILL do.

Use past tense 'markers' such as **letztes Jahr** (last year), **in der vorigen Saison** (last season), **als Kind** (as a child), **vor einigen Monaten** (a few months ago).

Now try this 🗣 SPEAKING

Answer these three questions. Say 2–3 sentences for each.

- Wie viel Sport treibst du jetzt?
- Wie viel Sport hast du letztes Jahr getrieben?
- Was wäre dein sportlicher Traum?

Here's a useful higher level phrase:
Mein Traum ist es, mein Land bei den Olympischen Spielen zu vertreten. It is my dream to represent my country at the Olympic Games.

Arranging to go out

Using Sie or du when arranging to go out? If you are unsure, use Sie until the person suggests using du.

Mit Freunden ausgehen

Möchtest du ...	Would you like to ...
einen Film sehen?	see a film?
schwimmen gehen?	go swimming?
zur Feier kommen?	come to the party?
Ich würde lieber ...	I would prefer to ...
in den Jugendklub gehen.	go to the youth club.
zum Skatepark gehen.	go to the skate park.
zu Hause bleiben.	stay at home.

Hast du am Samstag frei?
Are you free on Saturday?

Gehst du lieber ins Kino oder ins Konzert?
Do you prefer going to the cinema or to a concert?

Kaufst du die Eintrittskarten?
Are you buying the tickets?

Wann beginnt die Vorstellung?
When does the performance start?

weil (because)

weil + verb to END

Ich kann nicht kommen, weil ...	... ich dann Fußballtraining habe.
I can't come because ...	... I've got football training then.
	... ich kein Geld habe. ... I haven't got any money.
	... meine Eltern es nicht erlauben. ... my parents won't allow it.

Grammar page 93

Ich kann nicht kommen, weil ich Hausaufgaben machen muss.

 Worked example LISTENING 14 target C

Listen. Why can't Eva go to the film with her friends?
- **A** She can't afford it.
- **B** The time doesn't suit her.
- **C** She saw the film on Sunday.

Write the correct letter in the box. ☐ B

– Oh, je. Ich habe ein Problem! Ich habe gerade mein Taschengeld bekommen, also wollte ich mit meinen Freundinnen ins Kino gehen, aber die Vorstellung beginnt erst um neun Uhr und ich muss spätestens um zehn Uhr wieder zu Hause sein, weil ich am Sonntag früh aufstehen muss.

Learning vocabulary

To prepare for listening and reading exams, you need to learn lots of vocabulary.

- LOOK at and learn the words.
- COVER the English words.
- WRITE the English words.
- CHECK all the words.
- SEE how many you have got right.

 Now try this LISTENING 15 target C

Three people are talking about why they can't go out. What is their reason?
- **A** I am going to a wedding.
- **B** I haven't got any money.
- **C** I have got too much homework.
- **D** I would prefer to stay at home.
- **E** I need new shoes.

Write the correct letter in the box.

1 Vincenz ☐   **2** Tatjana ☐   **3** Patrik ☐

What I did last weekend

Use this page to learn some key past tense phrases to use in your speaking and writing.

Letztes Wochenende

Ich bin zu Hause geblieben.	I stayed at home.
Ich bin ins Kino gegangen.	I went to the cinema.
Ich bin in die Disko gegangen.	I went to the disco.
Ich war im Jugendklub.	I was at the youth club.
Ich habe Verwandte besucht.	I visited relatives.
Ich habe mich gut amüsiert.	I had a good time.
Ich habe mich gelangweilt.	I was bored.
Ich habe nichts Besonderes gemacht.	I didn't do anything special.
Ich habe mich ausgeruht.	I relaxed.
Ich habe im Geschäft gearbeitet.	I worked in the shop.

Question words

Grammar page 106

Wann?	When?
Warum?	Why?
Was?	What?
Wer?	Who?
Wie?	How?
Wo?	Where?
Was für ...?	What sort of?
Wen? Wem?	Who(m)?
Wessen?	Whose?
Wie viele?	How many?

Ich war auf einer Feier.

Worked example

 LISTENING 16 — target B

Jennifer is talking about the weekend.
What exactly did she do on Saturday morning?
bought a jacket in the sales / for half price

– Hast du ein schönes Wochenende gehabt, Jennifer?
– Letzten Samstagvormittag war ich in der Stadt und ich habe eine Jacke zum halben Preis im Sommerschlussverkauf gekauft. Mit Petra bin ich dann am Nachmittag Rollschuh gelaufen.

Make sure you are familiar with the words for times: **Vormittag** (morning), **Nachmittag** (afternoon) and **Abend** (evening).

EXAM ALERT!

Sometimes in higher grade questions students do not answer in enough detail. For example, in this question, more detail is needed than 'went to town' or 'bought a jacket'. Jennifer mentions the sales and the reduction to the jacket, so that needs to be in the answer.

Students have struggled with exam questions similar to this – **be prepared!**

Now try this

 LISTENING 17 — target B

Listen to the rest of the dialogue and answer the questions in English.

(a) What was Jennifer celebrating on Saturday evening?
(b) What exactly did Jennifer do on Saturday evening?
(c) What exactly did Jennifer's grandmother want to do on Sunday?
(d) Why exactly did Jennifer stay at home?

You need to be precise in your answers for questions like these – listen carefully for the details.

TV programmes

When reading or listening to passages about TV programmes, time phrases such as those below can all help you identify the tense.

Fernsehsendungen

Ich sehe gern ...	I like watching ...
Krimis (mpl)	detective shows
die Nachrichten (fpl)	the news
Dokumentarfilme (mpl)	documentaries
Seifenopern (fpl)	soap operas
Zeichentrickfilme (mpl)	cartoons
Sendungen (fpl) / Programme (npl)	(TV) programmes
Serien (fpl)	series
Satellitenfernsehen (n)	satellite TV
die Werbung	adverts
Zuschauer (m)	viewer

Tense markers

Grammar page 107

Past tense

als kleines Kind	as a small child
früher	previously, in the past
gestern	yesterday
letzte Woche	last week

Present tense

heute	today
heutzutage	these days
jetzt	now
normalerweise	normally

Future tense

in der Zukunft	in future
morgen (früh)	tomorrow (morning)
nächste Woche	next week
übermorgen	the day after tomorrow

Ich sehe mir gern Zeichentrickfilme an.

Worked example

READING   target **B**

Read Nermina's blog. What is a positive and negative aspect of TV, according to her?

Positive: relaxing

Negative: music programmes come on late at night

Normalerweise schalte ich immer den Fernseher nach der Schule ein und ich sehe eine Musiksendung, weil ich das sehr entspannend finde. Wir haben kein Satellitenfernsehen bei uns zu Hause, also nehme ich immer die Musiksendungen auf, weil sie oft erst spät in der Nacht im Fernsehen kommen.

EXAM ALERT!

Some students didn't give enough detail for the negative aspect here. If you are aiming higher, you need to write down the detail, not just the general gist. Here, you would have needed to mention the type of programmes that come on late at night – music shows.

Students have struggled with exam questions similar to this – **be prepared!**

Watch out for separable verbs that get split up in sentences. **Schalte ich ... ein** (turn on) **sehe mir ... an** (watch) and **nehme ... auf** (record).

Now try this

READING   target **B**

Read the rest of the blog. What positive and negative aspects of TV does Nermina mention?

Seit der Grundschule bin ich ein großer Fernsehfan und sehe mir gern fast alles an – Zeichentrickfilme finde ich immer sehenswert, weil ich gern lache. Ich finde es aber schade, dass man heute für viele Sportsendungen extra bezahlen muss. Auch wenn man die neusten Filme sehen will, muss man zu viel zahlen.

Cinema

Don't get bogged down in recounting every detail of a film in your speaking or writing assessment – give a brief outline of the plot and then lots of opinions.

Kino

Ich habe im Kino X gesehen.
I saw X at the cinema.

Es war ein Abenteuerfilm / Horrorfilm / Liebesfilm.
It was an adventure / horror / love film.

Es ging um Liebe / Familie.
It was about love / family.

Es war aufregend / blöd.
It was exciting / silly.

Die Geschichte war kompliziert / romantisch.
The story was complicated / romantic.

Der Film spielte in Köln.
The film was set in Cologne.

mit Untertiteln
subtitled

Ich habe einen Horrorfilm gesehen.

Imperfect tense

Grammar page 102

ist	➡	war	(is / was)
hat	➡	hatte	(has / had)
geht	➡	ging	(goes / went)
spielt	➡	spielte	(plays / played)
fährt	➡	fuhr	(drive / drove)
kauft	➡	kaufte	(buys / bought)

Im Film ging es um Freiheit / Geld / ein Verhältnis.
The film was about freedom / money / a relationship.

Worked example

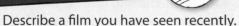

WRITING

Describe a film you have seen recently.

Ich gehe ziemlich oft ins Kino, obwohl das sehr teuer ist. Manchmal lade ich einen Film aus dem Internet herunter, aber ich finde Filme auf der breiten Leinwand im Kino viel spannender.

AIMING HIGHER

Der letzte Film, den ich mir angesehen habe, hieß „Am Waldrand". Es war ein Horrorfilm und er war sehr gruselig. Es ging um eine Clique, die in einem dunklen, alten Haus am Waldrand eine Geburtstagsparty feierte, aber jede Stunde ist irgendwie ein Jugendlicher verschwunden. Der Film war eigentlich ziemlich blöd und unglaubhaft, aber er war trotzdem unterhaltsam und die Spezialeffekte waren erstklassig.

irgendwie – somewhere
unglaubhaft – hard to believe
unterhaltsam – entertaining

Writing tips

- Make the description of the plot as clear and concise as possible; do not make it too complex.
- Make a plan for any writing you are preparing on a topic, even if it is just a small section of your overall piece.

General habits ➡ How often? ➡
Title? ⬅ Specific film ⬅ Opinion?
⬇ Genre? ➡ Plot? ➡ Opinion?

This is an example of a good written answer because of the amount of complex information and structures, including:
- a variety of tenses
- **es ging um** phrase
- a relative clause, **es ging um eine Clique, die ...**
- interesting vocabulary.

Now try this

WRITING

Use the flowchart and the text above to describe a film you have seen recently. Write about 200 words in German.

Music

Whether you are never without your earphones or prefer to play in an orchestra, music is a good topic to include in your assessments.

Die Musik

Ich höre gern Popmusik.
I like listening to pop music.
Rockmusik ist meine Lieblingsmusik.
Rock is my favourite music.
Die Melodie ist sehr wichtig.
The tune is very important.
Ich höre Musik auf meinem Handy.
I listen to music on my mobile phone.
Ich lade viel Musik aus dem Internet herunter.
I download a lot of music from the internet.
Ich gehe selten auf Konzerte.
I rarely go to concerts.
Die Tänzer waren wunderbar.
The dancers were wonderful.
Ich höre gern Radio.
I like listening to the radio.

Favourite things

Use Lieblings- + any noun (lower case) to talk about favourite things.

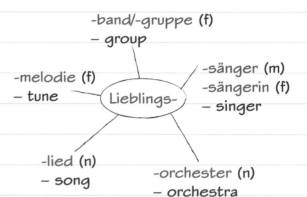

-band/-gruppe (f) – group
-melodie (f) – tune
Lieblings-
-sänger (m) -sängerin (f) – singer
-lied (n) – song
-orchester (n) – orchestra

Worked example

 target F-G

Which instrument does Daniel play?

Seit drei Monaten spiele ich Klavier.

 A   B   C

Write the correct letter in the box.
Daniel ☐ B

Reading tips

- Ignore all extra material – here the time phrase Seit drei Monaten (for three months) is irrelevant to the question.
- Try to remember the German word for each picture.
- Activities like these rely on vocabulary you probably learnt at the start of your German course – it shows just how important it is to revise and remember these topic areas.

Now try this

  target F-G

Which instrument do these three people play?

Max
Ich spiele im Orchester Klarinette.

Pia-Maria
Im Moment lerne ich Gitarre, aber ich finde das kompliziert.

Martin
In der Schule spielen wir Schlagzeug.

A   B   C   D   E

Complete the table by writing the correct letter.

Max	
Pia-Maria	
Martin	

25

New technology

Use time phrases to add interest to your description of online activities.

Aktivitäten online

Ich lade Fotos hoch.
I upload photos.

Ich lade Musik herunter
I download music.

Ich surfe im Internet.
I surf the internet.

Ich chatte online mit Freunden.
I chat to my friends online.

Ich sehe mir Videoclips an.
I watch video clips.

Ich besuche Chatrooms.
I visit chatrooms.

dürfen (to be allowed to) Grammar page 98

Dürfen is a modal verb so it needs an infinitive.

Ich darf nicht nach 22:00 Uhr auf dem Chat-Server sein.
I am not allowed to be on a chat room after 10 o'clock.
Ich darf keine Filme herunterladen.
I am not allowed to download films.

Worked example 🎧18 target A

Listen to Mia. Choose the correct statement.

A I love social network sites.
B My parents are fine about me going online.
C I never get on with my parents.

Write the correct letter in the box. ☐A☐

– Jeden Tag, wenn ich aus der Schule komme, schalte ich meinen Computer ein und gehe sofort in meinen Lieblingschat. Meine Eltern meinen, das ist wie eine Droge für mich, weil ich erst mit ihnen rede, wenn ich den Chatroom besucht habe! Darüber streiten wir uns oft.

Listening tips

• Don't worry about doing a simultaneous translation for yourself as you listen. Read the statements in advance and then focus on the parts of the recording that are RELEVANT to those statements.

• The more practice you have in LISTENING to German, the easier you will find it. Make sure you listen to all the recorded material supplied with this Revision Guide to give your listening skills a boost.

Now try this 🎧19 target A

Listen to the whole recording and choose the **three** correct statements.

A Mia is nosey.
B Mia is a passive user of social networks.
C Mia is not worried by her parents' threats.
D Mia needs the computer for schoolwork.

E Mia's parents don't care if she does her homework or not.
F Mia is never in a bad mood.

Write the **three** correct letters in the boxes. ☐ ☐ ☐

26

Language of the internet

The vocabulary here will help you become familiar with the language of the internet.

Internetsprache

Benutzer (m)	user
funktionieren	to work
Internetseite (f)	internet page
Nutzen (m)	use
Passwort (n)	password
speichern	to save, store
Technologie (f)	technology
Webseite (f)	web page

Ich gehe mit dem Handy ins Internet.
I go on the internet on my mobile.

Ich schreibe oft E-Mails.
I often write emails.

Ich chatte oft.
I often chat (online / MSN).

Ich lade (nie) Lieder herunter.
I (never) download songs.

Ich lade täglich Fotos hoch.
I upload photos every day.

Pluperfect tense

Grammar page 105

Pluperfect tense = HAD done something.

It is formed by using the imperfect form of haben / sein + past participle

Ich hatte es gedruckt.
I had printed it.

Sie war in den Urlaub gefahren.
She had gone on holiday.

Er hatte einen Computer gekauft, aber er wusste nicht, wie er funktionierte.
He had bought a computer but didn't know how it worked.

Worked example

Read the article. Answer the questions in English.

> Kevin war 14 Jahre alt, als seine Mutter ihm einen Computer kaufte. Der Junge hatte keinen einzigen Freund in der Schule und bevor er seinen Computer bekommen hatte, sah er abends immer alleine im Wohnzimmer fern oder er las Bücher über Flugzeuge.

Make sure you are familiar with irregular imperfect tense forms such as las (read) and sah ... fern (watched TV).

EXAM ALERT!

In activities like this, you have to come to a conclusion and give your opinion based on what you have read. There is often no definitive answer but you do need to write down an opinion that can be justified from the text.

Students have struggled with exam questions similar to this – **be prepared!**

What sort of a person is Kevin?

lonely / individual / quiet / withdrawn / unusual / unconventional

Give a reason for your choice.

He watches TV alone in the evenings or reads books about aeroplanes.

Now try this

Read the rest of the article and answer the questions in English.

(a) Why did Kevin's mother buy him a computer?

(b) Why was Kevin happy?

> Seine Mutter hoffte, dass ihr Sohn mit Hilfe des Internets Kontakt zu anderen jungen Leuten finden würde, die seine Interessen teilten. Sie hatte tatsächlich recht, weil er schnell zum täglichen Internetbenutzer wurde. Er fand immer mehr Internetseiten, wo er andere Jugendliche traf, die seine Meinungen teilten. Zum ersten Mal in seinem Leben fühlte Kevin sich glücklich.

Internet pros and cons

Be prepared to give positive and negative views of the internet by using the phrases here.

Vorteile und Nachteile

aktuell   up-to-date
lehrreich   educational
weltweit   worldwide

Es ist toll, dass ich Musik auf mein Handy herunterladen kann.
It's great I can download music to my mobile.
Ich benutze das Internet, um mit Freunden in Kontakt zu bleiben.
I use the internet to keep in touch with friends.
Internetseiten sind viel besser als altmodische Zeitschriften.
Web pages are much better than old-fashioned magazines.
Ich finde das Internet unterhaltsam.
I find the internet entertaining.

Das Internet kann für junge Kinder ein Risiko sein.
The internet can be a risk for young children.
Das Internet kann gefährlich sein.
The internet can be dangerous.
Computer können frustrierend sein.
Computers can be frustrating.

Using ob (whether)   Grammar page 93

ob = whether. It sends verb to the end:
Ich weiß nicht, ob er online ist.
I don't know whether he is online.

These conjunctions all send the verb to the end of the clause too:

dass	that	weil	because
obwohl	although	wenn	if

Das Internet ärgert mich, weil es so viele dumme Webseiten gibt.
I find the internet annoying because there are so many stupid web pages.

Das Internet macht süchtig.

Worked example WRITING

Write about the pros and cons of using a computer.

AIMING HIGHER Meiner Meinung nach sollten die Eltern dafür verantwortlich sein, dass ihre Kinder nicht das Risiko eingehen, computersüchtig zu werden. Obwohl ich mir ein Leben ohne Computer nicht vorstellen kann, weiß ich schon, wann die Bildschirmzeit zu Ende sein sollte und dass ich dann etwas anderes machen muss. Ich weiß, ich sollte seltener am Computer sitzen.

Aiming higher

✓ Use meiner Meinung nach (in my opinion) + imperfect modal.

✓ Include an idiom: das Risiko eingehen (to run the risk).

✓ Use obwohl, which sends the verb to the end.

✓ Include some interesting vocabulary by using words made up from more than one noun: Bildschirmzeit (screen time).

✓ Use higher level structures such as etwas anderes (something else), sich vorstellen (to imagine) + dative pronoun, and a comparative seltener (less often).

Now try this WRITING

Answer the questions to write a paragraph in German of about 100 words about your online life and opinions.

- How often are you online?
- What do you do online?
- What annoys you about online activities?
- What are the advantages of going online?

LEISURE

Had a look ☐   Nearly there ☐   Nailed it! ☐

Shops

Although the list of shops might look long, you'll be surprised at how many of them you already know because you recognise part of the word.

Geschäfte / Läden

 Friseur(salon) (m)

 Bäckerei (f)

 Blumenladen (m)

 Kleidungsgeschäft (n)

 Konditorei (f)

 Obst- und Gemüseladen (m)

 Supermarkt (m)

 Apotheke (f)

 Buchhandlung (f)

 Fleischerei / Metzgerei (f) butcher

 Kaufhaus (n) department store

 Lebensmittelgeschäft (n) grocer's

Definite article (the)

 Grammar page 85

Masculine nouns

nominative – der
Der Kiosk ist teuer.
↓
accusative – den
Ich finde den Kiosk teuer.

Feminine nouns

nominative and accusative – die
Die Bäckerei ist toll.
Ich finde die Bäckerei toll.

Neuter nouns

nominative and accusative – das
Das Kaufhaus ist preiswert.
Ich finde das Kaufhaus preiswert.

Look at how many of these shops end in the word for 'shop': das Geschäft or der Laden.

Worked example — READING — target G

What can you buy near here?
A Flowers
B Fruit
C Newspapers
Write the correct letter in the box. [B]

Obstmarkt

- Split the word into **Obst** (fruit) and the cognate **Markt** (market) and see if it reduces your answer options.
- Only A Flowers and B Fruit are likely to be bought at a market, so you now have to decide which it is.

Now try this — READING — target D-E

Which **three** shops did Elias visit yesterday?

Zuerst bin ich ins Musikgeschäft gegangen und dann bin ich ins Elektrogeschäft gegangen. Ich musste ein neues Radio kaufen. Am Ende bin ich in den Blumenladen gegangen. Meine Mutter feierte ihren 50. Geburtstag, und ich habe eine schöne Pflanze für sie gekauft.

A   B   C

D   E   F

Write the **three** correct letters in the boxes.

☐ ☐ ☐

29

Food shopping

Here are some food items and quantities it would be useful to learn.

Lebensmittel einkaufen

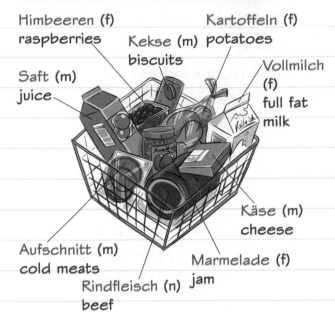

Himbeeren (f) raspberries

Kekse (m) biscuits

Kartoffeln (f) potatoes

Saft (m) juice

Vollmilch (f) full fat milk

Aufschnitt (m) cold meats

Rindfleisch (n) beef

Marmelade (f) jam

Käse (m) cheese

Quantities

Be careful not to use von (of) with quantities:

 eine Dose + Erbsen =

 a tin of peas

Here are a few more:

ein Dutzend	a dozen
ein Glas	a jar / glass of
eine Packung	a packet of
eine Scheibe	a slice of
eine Tafel	a bar of
eine Tüte	a bag of
ein Kilo	a kilo of

Worked example LISTENING 20 target B

Listen. Which statement describes Kerim's trip to the shops yesterday?

A He bought a different item from what he had planned.

B He thought the chocolate was expensive.

C The supermarket was some distance away.

Write the correct letter in the box. A

– Gestern Nachmittag bin ich in den Supermarkt nebenan gegangen, weil ich Lust auf Kekse hatte! Im Geschäft habe ich dann aber eine Tafel Schokolade im Sonderangebot gesehen, also habe ich sie mir gekauft. Sie hat nur €1,35 gekostet – sehr günstig, nicht?

Listening tips

- The question mentions 'yesterday' – be prepared to hear the PAST TENSE.

- Chances are you will hear something related to options A, B and C – don't be misled by hearing a key word as you have to understand what goes with the key word.

- DON'T PANIC – you have two chances to get all the information as you will hear the passage twice.

- JOT DOWN words in English or German when you are doing a listening task. You might find it helpful before you make your choice.

Small words are just as important as long ones! Here, the word **nebenan** (nearby) is enough to let you dismiss option C.

Now try this LISTENING 21 target B

Listen. Which statement describes Sophie's trip to the shops yesterday?

A She went out to buy some honey.

B She was surprised by the cost of the honey.

C Her mother was happy with the purchase.

Write the correct letter in the box. ☐

Beware of words that sound like English words but mean something different!

Shopping

Where there are shops, there's money, so make sure you are familiar with numbers in German (see page 108).

Das Einkaufen

Abteilung (f)	department
Auswahl / Wahl (f)	choice
Bankkarte (f)	bank card
Bargeld (n)	cash
Einkaufskorb (m)	shopping basket
Einkaufswagen (m)	shopping trolley
Kasse (f)	till / checkout
Kleingeld (n)	change, small coins
Konto (n)	bank account
Preis (m)	price
Schaufenster (n)	shop window
billig	cheap
günstig	low priced / value for money
herabgesetzt	reduced

Money

100 Cents = 1 Euro

 ein 10-Euro-Schein

 ein 2-Euro-Stück

Be careful with -zehn and -zig numbers in prices.

fünfzehn = 15	fünfzig = 50
siebzehn = 17	siebzig = 70

If you are noting down a price you hear, make sure you get the numbers the right way round:

vierunddreißig = 4 + 30 = 34

Write the 30 **before** the 4, even though you hear **vier** first.

Worked example SPEAKING

Gehst du oft einkaufen?

Ich gehe nicht sehr oft einkaufen, weil ich das langweilig finde. Letzte Woche bin ich ins Einkaufszentrum gegangen, aber ich habe nichts gekauft. Meiner Meinung nach war alles zu teuer.

AIMING HIGHER

Ja, aber ich kaufe jetzt lieber online als in der Stadt ein. Als ich vor einigen Wochen in der Innenstadt war, habe ich im Schaufenster des Elektrogeschäfts einen stark reduzierten MP3-Spieler gesehen und bin sofort hineingegangen, um ihn zu kaufen. Ich war aber sehr enttäuscht, als der Ladenbesitzer mir sagte, dass der MP3-Spieler reserviert war. Seitdem kaufe ich immer im Internet ein, weil dort die Auswahl viel besser ist!

CONTROLLED ASSESSMENT

Students who are aiming higher need to do more than just answer any given question in the speaking assessment. These students reply to the question first of all, and then both go on to expand and include further ideas.

This student is aiming higher by using:
- **als, da, dass, weil** structures
- an interesting past time phrase **bin ... hineingegangen** (went in)
- an adverb **sofort** (immediately)
- adjectives with correct endings **einen stark reduzierten MP3-Spieler**
- an **um ... zu ...** phrase
- past, future and present tenses.

Now try this SPEAKING

Gehst du oft einkaufen? Answer the question in 4–5 sentences.

Look at the second speaking example above and try to incorporate at least **three** of the elements into your text.

Clothes and colours

Learn clothes words with their gender, so you can make your adjectives agree.

Kleidung

der Hut
die Bluse
die Jacke
der Pullover / Pulli
der Rock
der Schuh

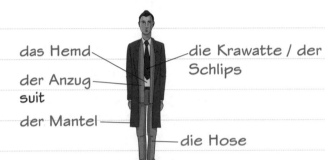

das Hemd
die Krawatte / der Schlips
der Anzug suit
der Mantel
die Hose

Adjective agreements

Grammar page 89

Masculine nouns

nom	acc	dat	
ein roter	einen roten	einem roten	Pulli

Feminine nouns

nom / acc	dat		
eine grüne	einer grünen	Krawatte Mütze	

Neuter nouns

nom / acc	dat		
ein blaues	einem blauen	Hemd	

Farben

 blau   gelb   lila   weiß    gestreift

 grün   rot   rosa   schwarz    kariert

Worked example

LISTENING 22   target F

What did Marlene buy at the boutique?

A   B   C

Write the correct letter in the box. C

– Was hast du gekauft, Marlene?
– Eine Hose.

EXAM ALERT!

Clothing is a topic many students feel confident with, but silly mistakes can still be made. For example, students often forget what **Hose** (trousers) means. Make sure you learn basic vocabulary like the words above so you don't get caught out.

Students have struggled with exam questions similar to this – **be prepared!**

Now try this

LISTENING 23   target F

Write the correct letters in the boxes for these girls.

A   B   C   D   E

1 Daniela   **2** Leona   **3** Ida

Buying clothes

If you give an opinion on clothes, make sure you justify it with REASONS.

Kleidung kaufen

anprobieren	to try on
bequem	comfortable
einkaufen gehen	to go shopping
Geschenk (n)	present
Größe (f)	size
Kleidung (f)	clothing
Marke (f)	brand
modisch / schick	fashionable
Schlange stehen	to queue
schön	lovely
sich umziehen	to change
Umkleidekabine (f)	changing room

Die Jacke ist mir zu groß.

Die Hose ist mir zu klein.

Accusative prepositions
Grammar page 86

The following prepositions are followed by the accusative case:

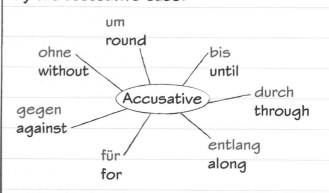

um – round
ohne – without
bis – until
durch – through
gegen – against
Accusative
entlang – along
für – for

(m) der Pulli – ohne **den** Pulli (der ➡ den) without the jumper

(f) die Mutter – für **die** Mutter (no change) for the mother

(n) das Geschäft – durch **das** Geschäft (no change) through the shop

(pl) die Geschenke – für **die** Geschenke (no change) for the presents

Worked example

WRITING target C–A

Write about buying clothes.

Ich liebe Mode. Ich gehe auf dem Flohmarkt einkaufen.

> This is correct writing, but look how just a few additions can raise its level ...

Ich liebe Mode und ich gehe oft auf den Flohmarkt, um schicke Klamotten zu kaufen.

> This is improved by adding:
> • a connective (**und**)
> • a time expression (**oft**)
> • an **um ... zu ...** phrase.

AIMING HIGHER

Seit meiner Kindheit liebe ich Mode und ich gehe heute immer noch oft auf den Flohmarkt, um mir klassische Klamotten auszusuchen, weil ich sie viel günstiger und interessanter als Markenkleidung finde. Eines Tages werde ich hoffentlich Modedesignerin sein – das ist mein Traum.

> To improve your writing still further, also try to add:
> • more interesting time phrases (**immer noch heute / eines Tages**)
> • a **weil** phrase offering a reason
> • a comparison
> • a future tense.

Now try this

WRITING

Write 100 words in German about your views on buying clothes. Include details of a recent shopping experience.

> Use connectives, a time expression and an **um ... zu** phrase, as well as at least **two** tenses.

Returning clothes

Returning clothes is another topic where it is useful to know a variety of tenses.

Kleidung zurückbringen

aus Baumwolle / Kunststoff	cotton / man-made fabric
beschädigt	damaged
kaputt	broken
schmutzig	dirty
eng / kurz / lang	tight / short / long
(un)zufrieden	(un)satisfied
enttäuscht	disappointed
Quittung (f)	receipt
Rabatt (m)	reduction
reparieren	to repair
schlechte Qualität	poor quality
Ich möchte das Geld zurück.	I would like the money back.
Es passt mir nicht gut.	It doesn't fit me well.
Es steht mir.	It suits me.
zurück	back
zurücknehmen	to take back
zurückkommen	to come back
zurückstellen	to put back
zurückfahren	to drive back

Es passt / steht mir

Some verbs use a dative pronoun mir, dir, ihm, ihr, uns, ihnen, meaning 'to me / you', etc.

Der Rock passt mir nicht.
The skirt doesn't fit me.

Die Stiefel stehen ihm gut.
The boots really suit her.

Worked example   LISTENING 24   target B

Klara is at a department store.

A She is pleased with her purchase.
B She is complaining about a purchase.
C She wants to try something on.

Write the correct letter in the box. ☐ B

– Ich habe gestern diesen Rock bei Ihnen gekauft. Als ich ihn heute Morgen anziehen wollte, habe ich bemerkt, dass er schmutzig war.

Listening tips

- Use your 5-minute reading time before your listening assessment wisely – the first sentence informs you of the topic area you are going to hear about. Here, it is shopping.

- When you have multiple choice options, you can learn more about what you are going to hear. Read the A, B, C options and you will find out you need to listen for information about whether Klara is pleased or not, or whether she wants to try an item on.

Now try this   LISTENING 25   target B

Listen to the rest of the recording and choose the correct answer.

1 Why can't Klara get her money back immediately?
  A The skirt is not faulty.
  B She has left the skirt at home.
  C She hasn't got her receipt. ☐

2 Why does she need the skirt?
  A She has a job interview next week.
  B She has a job interview tomorrow.
  C She always has to look good. ☐

Shopping opinions

If you want to discuss shopping in your writing and speaking assessments, include examples of online purchases along with traditional shopping.

Meinungen über das Einkaufen

Einkaufen kann ich nicht leiden.
I can't stand shopping.

Geschäfte interessieren mich sehr / nicht.
I find shops very / not at all interesting.

Ich habe nie / immer Lust, einkaufen zu gehen.
I never / always want to go shopping.

Online Einkaufen bietet mehrere Vorteile.
Online shopping offers several advantages.

Ich kaufe gern online ein, weil es eine bessere Auswahl an Produkten gibt.
I like shopping online because there is a better range of products.

Ich finde Einkaufszentren besser als kleine Geschäfte.
I find shopping centres better than small shops.

Um … zu…

Grammar page 94

This means 'in order to'.

comma + um + nouns / adjectives, etc. + zu + verb:

Man muss viele Geschäfte besuchen, **um** hübsche Sachen **zu** finden.
You have to visit a lot of shops to find nice things.

Ich gehe einkaufen, **um** Kleidung **zu** kaufen.
I go shopping in order to buy clothes.

Worked example

What is Dominik's opinion of online shopping?

> Als junger Mensch bin ich natürlich froh, dass ich rund um die Uhr Einkäufe machen kann, und das mache ich auch! Manchmal kommt es vor, dass ich noch bis spät in die Nacht Produkte online kaufe und erst beim Morgenlicht bemerke, dass diese vollkommen nutzlos sind.

Write **P** if it is positive. Write **N** if it is negative.
Write **P + N** if it is both.

P+N

- **froh** (happy) is a positive adjective, but don't jump to conclusions. Read on and you discover a negative aspect with products that are **nutzlos** (useless).

- If you are aiming higher, you are going to have to cope with some unfamiliar vocabulary in reading texts. Words such as **beim Morgenlicht** (at morning light) you can work out as meaning first thing in the morning.

Now try this

What are these people's opinions of online shopping?

Write **P** if it is positive.   Write **N** if it is negative.   Write **P + N** if it is both.

(a) Ich habe erst einmal etwas online gekauft. Das war ein Wecker für meine Mutter und er sah auf der Webseite toll aus. Als er zwei Tage später mit der Post geliefert wurde, war ich sehr enttäuscht, weil er viel kleiner als auf dem Internetbild war und die Uhrzeit selber war gar nicht einfach zu lesen. ☐

(b) Wir führen ein autofreies Leben und für meine Familie ist es sehr praktisch, alle Lebensmittel online zu bestellen. Der Supermarkt liefert sie dann direkt an die Tür und so spart man Geld und Zeit und hat weniger Ärger. ☐

Pocket money

Make sure you can talk about your pocket money – use the transcripts from this page for ideas (all transcripts available on www.pearsonschools.co.uk/mflrevisionaudio).

Taschengeld

Kreditkarte (f)   credit card

Portemonnaie (n)   wallet

Sparkasse (f)   savings bank

Meine Eltern geben mir 10 Pfund pro Woche.
My parents give me £10 a week.

Ich bekomme 30 Pfund pro Monat.
I get £30 a month.

Ich gebe mein Geld für … aus.
I spend my money on …

Kleidung   clothes

Komikhefte   comics

Schmuck   jewellery

Ich spare auf einen Computer / ein Fahrrad / ein Handy.
I'm saving for a computer / bike / mobile phone.

Plurals

German nouns all have different plurals. You can look in a dictionary if you are unsure.

An online search for 'Spielzeug plural' gives you the answer instantly:

> Spielzeug (n) (Genitiv des Spielzeugs, **plural** die **Spielzeuge**) – toy

Ich gebe mein Geld für Süßigkeiten aus.
I spend my money on sweets.

Worked example  LISTENING 26   target B

Listen to Josef talking about his pocket money.
What does he say about it?

A I don't waste money on magazines.
B In return for pocket money I have to do jobs at home.
C My attitude to pocket money has changed.
D There's no point in saving money.
E I would like to have more control over my spending.
F My pocket money is paid into my bank.

Write the correct letter in the box. ☐ F

– Als ich klein war, habe ich kein Taschengeld bekommen, weil meine Eltern alles für mich gekauft haben. Als ich auf die Hauptschule ging, habe ich aber zum ersten Mal eine monatliche Summe auf mein Bankkonto bekommen.

Listening tips

• In this type of question, LOOK THROUGH all the answer options carefully before you listen and try to PREDICT what language you are likely to hear.

• Make sure you revise your TENSES – here option C is about an attitude that has changed, so be prepared to hear past tenses (what the attitude was) and the present tense (what the attitude is now).

Josef says **auf mein Bankkonto bekommen** (got money in my bank account) – this is the key phrase you need to hear to lead you to the correct answer.

Now try this LISTENING 27 target B

Listen and choose the correct statement for Kristin, Silas and Sandra.
Write the correct letter in the box.

1 Kristin ☐   2 Silas ☐   3 Sandra ☐

Holiday destinations

Think about where you like to go on holiday, then think of ways to justify your choice.

Ferienziele

Am liebsten mache ich Urlaub ...
I like staying most of all ...

| zu Hause | at home |
| bei Freunden | with friends |

auf dem
Land

an der
Küste

in den
Bergen

in einer
Stadt

in einem
Dorf

weil ...
because ...

man im See schwimmen kann.
you can swim in the lake.
es dort viel wärmer als in England ist.
it is much warmer there than in England.
meine Eltern in den Bergen gern wandern gehen.
my parents like walking in the mountains.

Accusative and dative prepositions

Grammar
page 87

an	on, to
auf	on, to
in	in, into

These use the DATIVE case when there is NO MOVEMENT involved.

Ich wohne im Ausland.   I live abroad.

Das Haus liegt am See.
The house is on the lake.

BUT if there is MOVEMENT towards a place, this signals the ACCUSATIVE case.

Ich fahre ins Ausland.
I am going abroad.
Ich fahre an die Küste.
I am going to the coast.

Am liebsten mache ich Urlaub an der Küste.
I like staying on the coast most of tall.

Worked example

WRITING

Where do you like to go on holiday?

In den Sommerferien fahren wir immer ins Ausland, weil es dort sonnig und warm ist. Ich fahre am liebsten nach Italien. Die Italiener finde ich sehr freundlich und das Essen ist lecker!

This includes an inverted sentence (fahren wir), a preposition ins Ausland (abroad) and a subordinating conjunction (weil). The student also gives an opinion and justifies it.

AIMING HIGHER

Da ich letztes Jahr in den Ferien zu Hause geblieben bin, fahre ich diesen Sommer an die Küste, damit ich viele Wassersportarten machen kann. Meiner Meinung nach ist ein Urlaub ohne Sport gar kein Urlaub und deshalb fahren wir an einen Ferienort, wo es einen Kinderklub gibt.

Aiming higher

✓ The second answer includes a variety of subordinating conjunctions, such as damit (so that) and wo (where).

✓ Tenses are a sure sign you are aiming higher, so make sure you use past, present and future tenses in your work.

Now try this

WRITING

Describe your favourite holiday destination in German, in about 100 words.

Holiday accommodation

Connectives, adjectives, tenses and conjunctions – four key things to consider when preparing for a written or speaking assessment on holidays.

Die Ferienunterkunft

Bauernhaus (n) / Bauernhof (m)	farmhouse
Campingplatz (m)	campsite
Ferienwohnung (f)	holiday flat
Gasthaus (n)	guest house
Hotel (n)	hotel
Jugendherberge (f)	youth hostel
Pension (f)	bed and breakfast place
Broschüre (f)	brochure
Unterkunft (f)	accommodation
Wohnwagen (m)	caravan, mobile home
Zelt (n)	tent
ankommen	to arrive
mieten	to hire, rent
übernachten	to stay the night
verbringen	to spend (time)
beliebt	popular

Using gern, lieber, am liebsten (like, prefer, like most of all)

A simple way of showing a preference is to use gern (like), lieber (prefer) and am liebsten (like most of all).

gern ♥
lieber ♥♥
am liebsten ♥♥♥

- Put gern and lieber after the verb:

  Ich schlafe gern im Freien.
  I like sleeping outdoors.

  Ich bleibe lieber im Hotel.
  I prefer staying in a hotel.

- Use am liebsten to start your sentence:

  Am liebsten zelte ich.
  Most of all I like camping.

Worked example SPEAKING target A

AIMING HIGHER

Wo übernachtest du im Urlaub am liebsten?

Am liebsten übernachte ich in einem Hotel mit Hallenbad und Fitnessraum, aber das kostet viel Geld, also mache ich das nur selten. Letzten Sommer haben wir in einer Pension übernachtet, aber das war schrecklich, weil wir abends um neun Uhr ins Bett gehen mussten. Diesen Sommer werden wir eine Ferienwohnung an der Küste mieten und ich freue mich sehr darauf. Ich bin immer dankbar, dass wir nicht im Zelt schlafen müssen, weil ich das unbequem, laut und kalt finde.

Aiming higher

Include the following in your speaking and writing to aim for the best possible answer.

1. ADJECTIVES make your speaking and writing much more ... fascinating, exciting, amusing.

2. Think PPF (past, present, future) TENSES before you say anything and then figure out a way to incorporate all three into your answer.

3. CONJUNCTIONS give lots of scope for great sentences, so make sure you are confident with weil, wenn and dass, and can also have a go with obwohl, bevor and wo.

 Now try this SPEAKING

Answer these questions as fully as you can. Talk for about **one** minute.

- Wo übernachtest du im Urlaub am liebsten?
- Warum?

 Include **connectives**, **tenses**, **adjectives** and **conjunctions** in your answers.

Booking accommodation

If you're booking accommodation, you can't avoid dates, so make sure you are confident with recognising and expressing them.

Eine Unterkunft reservieren

Aufenthalt (m)	stay
Einzelzimmer (n)	single room
Doppelzimmer (n)	double room
Mehrbettzimmer (n)	shared room
Zweibettzimmer (n)	twin room
Rezeption (f)	reception
Halbpension (f)	half-board
Vollpension (f)	full board
Aussicht (f) / Blick (m)	view
Balkon (m)	balcony
Reservierung (f)	reservation
Gast (m)	guest
buchen	to book
preiswert / günstig	value for money
reservieren	to reserve

Making a request

You can just ask for things by adding bitte to the end: Ein Einzelzimmer, bitte. But it's more polite to use a conditional sentence:

Ich möchte bitte ein Einzelzimmer reservieren.   I would like to reserve a single room.

Ich hätte gern ein Zimmer mit Balkon.   I would like a room with a balcony.

Wir möchten bitte ein Doppelzimmer reservieren.   We would like to reserve a double room.

Wir hätten gern ein Zimmer mit Halbpension.   We would like a room with half-board.

Saying dates

Vom ... bis ... (from ... to ...)

1st	ersten	7th	siebten
2nd	zweiten	12th	zwölften

If you are writing dates, add a full stop after the number: vom 1. bis zum 14. August.

Worked example   target E

Which booking matches this guest's requirements?

> Ich möchte bitte vom dritten bis zum dreizehnten Juli ein Einzelzimmer reservieren. Ich hätte, wenn möglich, gern ein Zimmer mit Balkon.

A A double room with sea view
B A single room with balcony
C A single room with dinner

Write the correct letter in the box. ☐ B

Reading tips

Doing a reading activity is like being a detective – look for the clues and solve the mystery!

• Look for the type of room first – Einzelzimmer, and you can immediately rule out option A as that has a double room.

• The remaining clue is either a balcony or a meal. Go back to the text to discover the words mit Balkon (with a balcony) and you've found the answer!

Now try this   target E

What does this guest request? Write the correct letter in the box.
A Two rooms on separate floors and parking
B Two rooms on the same floor and parking
C A family room and parking ☐

> Ich möchte bitte ein Zweibettzimmer für vier Nächte reservieren. Am liebsten hätte ich auch ein Doppelzimmer auf derselben Etage. Ich möchte bitte einen Parkplatz reservieren, wenn möglich.

Staying in a hotel

Hotels may not always crop up as a topic but much of the vocabulary on this page is also relevant for staying at a bed and breakfast or a youth hostel.

Im Hotel

Fitnessraum (m) — gym

Freibad (n) — outdoor pool

Garage (f) — garage

Hallenbad (n) — indoor pool

Klimaanlage (f) — air conditioning

Satellitenfernsehen (n) — satellite TV

Schlüssel (m) — key

mit Bad — with a bath

mit Blick auf — with a view of

mit Dusche — with a shower

Relative pronouns

Grammar page 94

Use a relative pronoun to describe somebody WHO is doing something.

Relative pronouns send the verb to the end of the clause, just like weil (because) and wenn (if).

(m)
Der Mann, der im Hotel übernachtet, sitzt oft auf dem Balkon. The man, who is staying in the hotel, often sits on the balcony.

(f)
Die Familie, die hier war, war sehr unfreundlich. The family, who was here, was very unfriendly.

(n)
Das Kind, das im Schwimmbad ist, kann sehr gut schwimmen. The child, who is in the pool, can swim very well.

Worked example

READING · *target B*

Complete the text with **one** of the words that follow.

> Die Reise im Sommer hat viel Spaß gemacht. Obwohl das Hotel nicht sehr luxuriös war, war das der _____ Sommeraufenthalt meines Lebens!

A längste   **B** beste   **C** schrecklichste
Write the correct letter in the box.   ☐B

- Use the gist of the text to identify that this person is speaking positively about the holiday, **hat viel Spaß gemacht**, so the answer is unlikely to be a negative adjective.
- You can't choose an adjective which is not referred to in the text – here there is no mention of the length of the holiday, so the missing word can't be option A.

Now try this

READING · *target B*

Read the rest of the holiday report.

Fill in the gaps in the text with words from below. Write the correct letter in the box.

A Familienzimmer   **F** sehen
B Unterkunft   **G** Nachteile
C putzen   **H** lag
D las   **I** Wohnwagen
E Hallenbad   **J** reservieren

> Das Hotel war modern und ☐ direkt am Strand, aber leider hatte es keinen Fitnessraum und das ☐ machte immer um sieben Uhr abends zu. Glücklicherweise gab es in unserem ☐ Satellitenfernsehen, also konnte mein kleiner Bruder immer noch seine Lieblingssendungen ☐. Am Ende des Aufenthalts haben wir alle versprochen, das Zimmer nächstes Jahr wieder zu ☐, weil es trotz der ☐ ein wunderschöner Urlaub war!

Staying on a campsite

Most of the vocabulary for this topic will also be useful for other types of holiday accommodation.

Auf dem Campingplatz

im Freien	in the open air
im Wohnwagen (m)	in a caravan
im Zelt (n)	in a tent
Schlafsack (m)	sleeping bag
Feld (n)	field
Freizeitpark (m)	theme park
Grill (m)	barbecue
Hügel (m)	hill
Insel (f)	island
Meer (n) / See (f)	sea
Natur (f)	nature
See (m)	lake
Spielplatz (m)	playground
Wald (m)	wood / forest
buchen	to book
reservieren	to reserve
wandern	to walk
zelten	to camp

Giving location details

Here are some ways of letting someone know where you live or are staying.

am	at / on
dort	there
entfernt	away from
hier	here
in der Nähe von	near to
neben	near

Der Campingplatz … The campsite …	liegt in der Nähe von Lindau. is near to Lindau.
	ist etwa 30 Gehminuten vom Stadtzentrum entfernt. is about 30 minutes on foot from the town centre.
	liegt am Bodensee. is on Lake Constance.
	befindet sich am Waldrand. is situated on the edge of the wood.

Worked example

LISTENING 28   **target A***

Listen to Julia. What event in May does she mention and why?

They opened a new boat house where you can hire boats / water skis.

– Ich freue mich sehr auf unseren Urlaub auf dem Campingplatz Maria am Bodensee. Laut der Broschüre wurde Ende Mai ein neues Bootshaus eröffnet, wo man jetzt Boote und Wasserskier mieten kann.

- Ignore language which is **not needed** for the question. Here, the first few words are 'padding' and can be ignored. They don't offer any information about an event in May.

- You must write down the **detail** for your answer if you are aiming higher. You need to say more than 'you can hire boats' – identify **exactly** what you can hire (boats and water skis) and why (they've opened a new boat house).

Now try this

LISTENING 29   **target A***

Listen to the rest of the recording.

(a) Why exactly has Julia already booked a place on a kayak course?

(b) Why is she particularly looking forward to the new shower facility?

(c) Which other improvement is Julia excited about?

(d) Why exactly?

> Make sure you give enough detail in your answers.

Had a look ☐   Nearly there ☐   Nailed it! ☐

Holiday activities

For more things you might do on holiday, look at the leisure activities on pages 19 and 20.

Urlaubsaktivitäten

Man kann …

Bergsteigen gehen

Eislaufen gehen

faul sein

Rad fahren

schwimmen gehen

segeln

Ski fahren

spazieren gehen

Tennis spielen

Saying what you can do

Grammar page 98

The verbs on the left are in the infinitive form – you need to use this form after the expression Man kann … (you can …).

Man kann … You can …	ins Freibad gehen. go to the pool.
	sich sonnen. sunbathe.

If you start your sentence with a time or place expression, kann and man swap places.

In den Alpen kann man …
In the Alps you can …

In den Ferien kann man reiten.
In the holidays you can go horse riding.

Worked example

READING   target E

Read this text about a holiday resort.

Im Schwarzwald

Hier kann man …
- Klettern ausprobieren.
- Wasserski lernen.
- im Wald spazieren gehen.
- einen Ausflug nach Freiburg machen.
- den Freizeitpark besuchen.

Which **two** activities are advertised?

A Day trips   **B** Cycling
C Skiing   **D** Walking

Write the **two** correct letters in the boxes.

A D

Dealing with unknown words

- The vocabulary in these sorts of reading tasks is all in the vocabulary list, but as you can't be expected to learn the entire list, you will have to rely on some reading strategies.
- Focus on what is key vocabulary and what is not – here the title Im Schwarzwald (in the Black Forest) is purely there to set the scene.
- Read the text, then look at the four options in English. Can you spot any answers straight away?
- Read the German words carefully – Wasserski is not option C (skiing) just because it ends with ski.

Now try this

READING   target E

Read the text again. Which **two** further activities are advertised?
A Entertainment evenings   **B** Climbing   **C** Rollercoasters   **D** Theme parks
Write the two correct letters in the boxes. ☐ ☐

Holiday preferences

What sort of holiday do you like – sporty, lazy, chilled? As well as saying what you DO enjoy doing, make sure you can say what you DON'T enjoy.

Thinking positively

Ich mache gern Urlaub in (Amerika).
I like going on holiday to (America).

Ich ziehe (Sporturlaube) vor.
I prefer (sports holidays).

Am liebsten (übernachte ich im Hotel).
Most of all (I like staying in a hotel).

Mein Lieblingsurlaub wäre (eine Woche in der Türkei).
My favourite holiday would be (a week in Turkey).

Urlaub mit Freunden finde ich …
I find holidays with friends …

ausgezeichnet	excellent
fantastisch	fantastic
herrlich	wonderful
super / spitze	super

Thinking negatively

Ich fahre nicht gern (ins Ausland).
I don't like going (abroad).

(Sporturlaube) kann ich nicht leiden.
I can't stand (sports holidays).

Ich würde nie auf Skiurlaub fahren.
I would never go on a skiing holiday.

(Eine Woche in der Sonne) interessiert mich nicht.
(A week in the sun) doesn't interest me.

Familienurlaub finde ich … I find family holidays …	… langweilig. … tiresome.
	… schlecht. … bad.
	… schrecklich. … terrible.

Worked example

LISTENING 30 **target A**

Kymete is talking about watersports holidays.
What does she say about them?

A They are good value.
B The weather is not important.
C The equipment is of a high standard.

Write the correct letter in the box. ☐C

– Ich fahre in den Ferien sehr gern ans Meer, weil ich Wassersportfan bin. Das kostet aber viel Geld, also darf ich das nur jedes zweite Jahr machen. Am liebsten segele ich, aber wenn der Wind nicht weht, macht es keinen Spaß, weil man nicht segeln kann. Ich finde, das Beste am Wassersporturlaub ist, dass die Boote immer super modern und sauber sind.

Listening tips

- ALL THREE answer options will be mentioned somewhere in the passage – your job is to understand in what context they are mentioned.
- If you do change your mind about an answer, make sure you CROSS it out completely and write the correct answer clearly instead.
- LISTEN for clues from the tone of the speaker's voice.

Now try this

LISTENING 31

Listen to Kodra, Annika and Matthias talking about holidays. What do they say about them?

1 Kodra ☐

A I don't enjoy the holidays.
B I don't mind staying at home in the holidays.
C I would like to go abroad.

2 Annika ☐

A I make friends on holiday.
B Our campsite is lovely.
C We always go to the same place.

3 Matthias ☐

A My brother and I are the same level at skiing.
B I dread the Christmas holidays.
C I always look forward to the Christmas holidays.

Holiday plans

Make sure you are confident with a few of the future expressions listed here, so you can include one in your written and speaking assessments on holiday plans.

Ferienpläne

Ich werde	I will ...
In den Ferien wird er ...	In the holidays he will ...
Hoffentlich werden sie ...	Hopefully they will ...
Eines Tages werden wir ...	One day we will ...
nach Australien fahren.	go to Australia.
auf Musiktour gehen.	go on a music tour.
meine Cousinen besuchen.	visit my cousins.
nächsten Sommer	next summer
nächsten Winter	next winter
nächstes Jahr	next year
in Zukunft	in the future
in zwei Jahren	in two years

Ich freue mich (sehr) darauf.
I am (really) looking forward to it.

Wenn ich älter bin, werde ich einen Ferienjob finden.
When I am older, I will find a holiday job.

Future tense

Grammar page 103

The future tense is formed by a part of **werden** (to become) + infinitive.

ich	werde
du	wirst
er / sie / man	wird
wir / Sie / sie	werden

Ich werde nach Ungarn fahren.
I will go to Hungary.

If you start your sentence with a time expression, **werde** and **ich** swap places.

Nächstes Jahr werde ich nach Amerika fahren.

Worked example

WRITING

What are your holiday plans for next year?

AIMING HIGHER

Nächsten Sommer werde ich mit meiner Familie nach Spanien fliegen und wir werden in einer luxuriösen Ferienwohnung an der Küste wohnen. Ich freue mich irrsinnig darauf, weil ich noch nie in Spanien gewesen bin, obwohl ich die Sprache seit drei Jahren in der Schule lerne. Wir werden einen Tagesausflug nach Barcelona machen, um die historischen Sehenswürdigkeiten dort zu besichtigen, aber ich fürchte, dass es mir zu heiß sein wird und ich bin mir sicher, dass ich lieber an der Küste bleiben werde.

CONTROLLED ASSESSMENT

Some students produced assessments with short and repetitive sentences. Much more impressive were those students who used a variety of structures, interesting vocabulary, a range of tenses and justified their opinions.

- This starts with the time phrase **Nächsten Sommer** and inverts the future tense correctly, so **werde** is the next word.
- Other notable expressions include **Ich freue mich darauf** + **weil** followed by the perfect tense and **ich fürchte / bin mir sicher, dass** ... plus the future tense.

Now try this

WRITING

Write 100 words in German about your holiday plans for next year.

If you give your opinion, justify it with a **weil** clause.

Past holidays

Make sure you can use the perfect tense when talking about holidays in the past.

Vergangene Ferien

letzten Sommer	last summer
in den Winterferien	in the winter holiday
letztes Jahr	last year
vor zwei Jahren	two years ago

Ich habe eine Tour gemacht.
I went on a tour.

Ich habe in einer Jugendherberge übernachtet.
I stayed at a youth hostel.

Ich bin Ski gefahren.

Ich bin nach Rom geflogen.

Wir haben gezeltet.

Wir haben Klettern gemacht.

Das hat Spaß gemacht.

The perfect tense

Grammar page 100-101

Use the perfect tense to talk about the past.

ich habe		gekauft (bought)
du hast	**+**	gemacht (did)
er / sie / man hat		besucht (visited)
wir haben		gesehen (saw)
ich bin		gegangen (gone)
du bist	**+**	geflogen (flew)
er / sie / man ist		gefahren (went / drove)
wir sind		angekommen (arrived)

Use **Es war** to give an opinion in the past.

Es war...

spitze / wunderschön.

mies / furchtbar.

Worked example

LISTENING 32 target D

What did Djordje do last year on holiday?

A   B   C

D   E

Write the correct letter in the box. ☐ C

– Letzten Sommer bin ich mit meiner Familie in den Schwarzwald gefahren. Wir haben gezeltet, aber es war nachts furchtbar laut.

nachts – at night

Be prepared

- READ THE RUBRIC first: this is about 'last year', so you are going to hear past tense sentences.
- LOOK AT THE PICTURES and think about what German words you might expect to hear.
- REMEMBER – you will hear the extract TWICE, so don't panic if you don't get the answer first time round.

Now try this

LISTENING 33 target D

Listen and match three more people to their holiday activity. Choose from pictures A–E above.
Write the correct letter in the box.

1 Kuschtrin ☐   2 Bierta ☐   3 Romeo ☐

Countries

Learn countries and nationalities together. Many of them sound like English!

Länder

Country	Upper case! ↘	↘ Lower case! ↘	Adjective
Deutschland	der Deutsche / ein Deutscher	die / eine Deutsche	deutsch
England	Engländer	Engländerin	englisch
Frankreich	Franzose	Französin	französisch
Großbritannien	Brite	Britin	britisch
Irland	Ire	Irin	irisch
Italien	Italiener	Italienerin	italienisch
Österreich	Österreicher	Österreicherin	österreichisch
Schottland	Schotte	Schottin	schottisch
Spanien	Spanier	Spanierin	spanisch
Wales	Waliser	Waliserin	walisisch
die Schweiz	Schweizer	Schweizerin	schweizerisch
die Türkei	Türke	Türkin	türkisch
die Vereinigten Staaten	Amerikaner	Amerikanerin	amerikanisch

Worked example

Write about where you and your family are from.

AIMING HIGHER Obwohl ich Irin bin, habe ich nie in Irland gewohnt, weil ich in London geboren bin. Mein Vater ist Ire, aber meine Mutter kommt aus Südafrika. Sie haben sich an der Uni in London kennengelernt und nach dem Studium haben sie in der Hauptstadt Arbeit gefunden. Sie wollten nicht in ihre Heimatländer zurückkehren und deshalb wohnen wir in London, einer multikulturellen Stadt, die ich liebe.

Aiming higher

For a higher grade, try to include:

1. a VARIETY of prepositions + correct endings
2. a subordinating conjunction obwohl (although)
3. er and sie forms, to allow for the use of ist (is) rather than bin (am);
4. an imperfect modal verb + negative Sie wollten nicht
5. confident control of word order, shown by deshalb (therefore) + verb next.

Now try this

Write 60 words in German about where you come from.

- Welche Nationalität hast du? (Und deine Eltern?)
- Wo wurdest du geboren und wo wohnst du jetzt?

Use the **past** tense to describe where you were born, then the **present** for where you live now.

My house

You will have met this topic at Key Stage 3 – test yourself to make sure you remember!

Mein Haus

Doppelhaus (n)	semi-detached house
Einfamilienhaus (n)	detached house
Wohnblock (m)	block of flats
Wohnung (f)	flat
im Erdgeschoss	on the ground floor
im zweiten Stock	on the second floor
auf der ersten Etage	on the first floor

Der, die, das, die

Grammar page 85

Three genders and a plural make up the German words for 'the'.

der – masculine	
die – feminine	die – all plurals
das – neuter	

If two or more German words are combined it is the LAST word which gives the whole word its gender.

Kleider (npl) + Schrank (m) ➡
DER Kleiderschrank (m) – cupboard

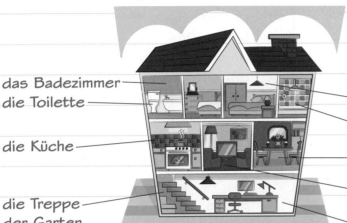

das Badezimmer
die Toilette
die Küche
die Treppe
der Garten

das Schlafzimmer
die Dusche
das Esszimmer
das Wohnzimmer
das Arbeitszimmer

Worked example

  target C-D

Read the text.

Sabine: Unser Haus ist klein. Es ist ein Einfamilienhaus. Seit drei Jahren wohnen wir hier. Wir haben eine schöne Küche, aber keine Dusche. Das finde ich ärgerlich.

(a) What type of property does Sabine live in?   detached house

(b) What does she find annoying?
not having a shower

EXAM ALERT!

In this type of question you need to note details. Make sure you read the question carefully to see what you need to find, and only give the information you are asked for. Don't be tempted to write lots of extra information, even if you are pleased you have understood it.

> Students have struggled with exam questions similar to this – **be prepared!**

Now try this

  target C-D

Read the text and answer the questions for Hugo.

Hugo: Wir wohnen in einer Wohnung am Stadtrand. Die Wohnung ist im siebten Stock, aber glücklicherweise muss man die Treppen nur benutzen, wenn der Aufzug nicht funktioniert. Der Nachteil der Wohnung ist, dass man keinen Garten hat, aber der Stadtpark ist in der Nähe.

(a) What type of property does Hugo live in?
(b) What makes up for not having a garden?

My room

Using prepositions correctly when talking about your room will help you aim for a higher level.

Mein Zimmer

Boden (m)	floor
Decke (f)	blanket
Etagenbett (n)	bunk bed
Fenster (n)	window
Möbel(stück) (n)	furniture
Schublade (f)	drawer
Wand (f)	wall

der Schreibtisch
das Bücherregal
das Kopfkissen
der Schrank
der Spiegel
der Vorhang
das Bild
die Lampe das Bett der Sessel

Dative prepositions

aus	from	nach	after
außer	except	seit	since
bei	at	von	from
mit	with	zu	to

- (m) der Sessel ➡ zu dem / zum Sessel

  (der ➡ dem) – to the floor

- (f) die Kommode ➡ aus der Kommode

  (die ➡ der) – from the chest of drawers

- (n) das Regal ➡ von dem / vom Regal

  (das ➡ dem) – from the shelf

- (pl) die Pflanzen ➡ mit den Pflanzen

  (die ➡ den + -n) – with the plants

Worked example 🎧 34 target B

Listen. How could Joachim's room be better?

A Be on the first floor.
B Have bunk beds.
C Have a bigger window.

Write the correct letter in the box. B

Just because you hear the word **Fenster**, it does not necessarily mean that answer C is correct. You have to understand what is said about the window.

– Mein Zimmer ist im ersten Stock und es ist ziemlich groß und hell. Ich teile mir das Zimmer mit meinem Bruder, aber es wäre besser, wenn wir ein Etagenbett hätten. Mit zwei Betten im Zimmer kann man nicht einmal das Fenster aufmachen, weil die Betten es blockieren.

EXAM ALERT!

Students often think the answer to listening tasks is in the final part – as that is what they remember the best. In tasks like this, the answer could be anywhere, so you have to concentrate and understand everything, from the beginning to the end.

Students have struggled with exam questions similar to this – **be prepared!**

Now try this 🎧 35 target B

Listen to Georg and Anna. How could their rooms be improved? Write the correct letter in the box.

Georg's room

A Swap rooms with his sister. **B** Buy a desk. **C** Paint the walls. ☐

Anna's room

A Keep it tidy. **B** Change her curtains. **C** Have a pet. ☐

Helping at home

Don't forget to include time expressions like those below when talking about helping at home.

Im Haushalt helfen

Ich ...   I ...

babysitte.	babysit.
putze das Bad.	clean the bath.
mache das Bett.	make the bed.
gehe einkaufen.	go shopping.
mähe den Rasen.	mow the lawn.
wasche das Auto.	wash the car.
füttere die Haustiere.	feed the pets.

bringe mein Zimmer in Ordnung.
tidy my room.

leere die Spülmaschine.
empty the dishwasher.

stecke die Kleider in die Waschmaschine
put the clothes in the washing machine.

Time expressions

Grammar page 107

Add time expressions wherever you can.

ab und zu	now and again
dann und wann	now and then
immer	always
manchmal	sometimes
nie	never
oft	often
selten	seldom

Remember to make sure the verb always comes in second place:
Ich decke **manchmal** den Tisch.
I sometimes lay the table.
but **Manchmal** decke ich den Tisch.

Worked example

Wie hilfst du im Haushalt?

Wenn man ab und zu im Haushalt helfen will, zum Beispiel beim Rasenmähen, sollte man das zuerst mit den Eltern besprechen, sodass man nichts Falsches macht.

AIMING HIGHER Vor zwei Monaten haben meine Eltern mich gebeten, öfter im Haushalt zu helfen, weil ich, ihrer Meinung nach, zu faul geworden bin. Ich sollte hilfsbereiter sein, sonst würde ich kein Taschengeld bekommen. Das fand ich unfair, aber am Tag danach bin ich besonders früh aufgestanden, um den Frühstückstisch zu decken und Kaffee zu kochen.

Liven up any present tense sentences with interesting conjunctions and structures, **zum Beispiel** (for example), **etwas Falsches** (something wrong).

Talk about a particular experience to make sure you have a past tense in your work, **vor zwei Monaten** (two months ago).

Speaking tip

Don't learn your answers off by heart in a set order, as your teacher may ask slightly different questions in random order. Make sure you listen carefully to the question and answer appropriately.

Now try this

Prepare answers to these questions in German. Say 4–5 sentences about each.

• Wie oft hilfst du im Haushalt?   • Wie hilfst du?   • Wie findest du das?

Where I live

Use the vocabulary here to talk about the area around where you live in more detail.

Wo ich wohne

Ich wohne ...   I live ...
  in der Hauptstadt.   in the capital city.
  in der Stadtmitte.   in the town centre.
  in einem Dorf.   in a village.
Die Gegend ist historisch / industriell.
The area is historic / industrial.
Die Landschaft ist flach / herrlich.
The landscape is flat / magnificent.
Es gibt zehntausend Einwohner.
There are 10,000 inhabitants.
Es ist von .... umgeben.
It is surrounded by ...

Revising grammar

- Many of the reading exercises are made easier if you have a sound grammatical knowledge. It's well worth revising grammar to give you a solid foundation for tackling a variety of reading passages.

- Use the complete grammar section at the back of this guide (page 85). After revising a few topic pages, turn to the grammar section and revise a couple of pages there.

Autobahnen
motorways

Bäumen
trees

Bergen
mountains

Gebäuden
buildings

Fabriken
factories

Wiesen
meadows

Worked example

Complete the text with one of the words that follow.

> Ich war viel glücklicher, als wir auf dem Land wohnten. Jetzt wohnen wir in einer hässlichen, industriellen Gegend, weil meine Mutter hier bei einer technischen Firma arbeitet. Statt von Bäumen und Wiesen ist unser Haus von vielen _____ umgeben.

Write the correct letter in the box.

A Feldern   **B** Fabriken   **C** Flüssen

☐ B

Tips for gapped exercises

- Look at each sentence and try to work out the meaning first of all.

- It is sometimes difficult to work out the meaning of an isolated word, such as the options, as you have no context to help you, so ensuring you know a wide RANGE OF VOCABULARY will certainly help you for this activity type.

- If you do understand an option and know it doesn't make sense in the sentence, cross it out, so you only have two choices to work with.

Now try this

Now complete these sentences. Write the correct letter in each box.

(a) Ich finde die Tausenden Stadtbesucher sehr nervig. Im Sommer kommen Tausende Touristen hierher, und sie _____ oft ihren Abfall auf den Bürgersteig. Das finde ich schrecklich.

  A vorbereiten   **B** werfen   **C** decken   ☐

(b) Nachts kann es hier recht laut sein, weil wir von Bahnlinien und Autobahnen umgeben sind. Im Gegensatz dazu bin ich tagsüber in meiner Schule am Stadtrand, wo alles viel _____ ist.

  A ruhiger   **B** schmutziger   **C** lebendiger   ☐

Places in town

Places in town may be familiar but check details such as spelling and gender carefully.

In der Stadt

 Bahnhof (m)   Bibliothek (f)   Dom (m)

 Fitnesszentrum (n)   Kino (n)

 Kirche (n)   Spielplatz (m)

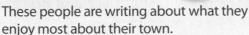

Einkaufszentrum (n)
shopping centre

Rathaus (n)
town hall

Es gibt ... (there is / are ...)

Use *es gibt* + accusative (*einen, eine, ein*) in different tenses to help improve your speaking and writing.

Es gibt ... ➡ present – There is ...

Als ich klein war, gab es ... ➡ imperfect – When I was young, there was ...

Vorher hatte es ... gegeben. ➡ pluperfect – Earlier there had been ...

In Zukunft wird es ... geben. ➡ future – In future there will be ...

In meiner idealen Stadt würde es ... geben. ➡ conditional – In my ideal town there would be ...

... *eine Eishalle*

Worked example

 target C-D

These people are writing about what they enjoy most about their town.

Klaus Ich bin Sportler und für mich ist das Freizeitzentrum mit Hallenbad das Beste hier.

Petra Ich bin ein großer Filmfan. Das neue Kino in der Innenstadt hat alle neuesten Kinohits.

Stefan Ich studiere Geschichte an der Uni und für mich ist die Stadt ideal. Ich besuche oft die historischen Gebäude in der Altstadt.

Ben Ich gehe sehr gern einkaufen. Am Wochenende bin ich immer im Einkaufszentrum zu finden.

Write the initial of the person: **K** (Klaus), **P** (Petra), etc.

Who is studying history? ⬚ S

Answering 'Who?' questions

- There might be more people to choose from than are needed. Your job is to track down the RELEVANT SENTENCE for each question.

- People can be used MORE THAN ONCE as the answer, so don't discount someone because they have already been the answer.

- Although an obvious point, make sure you write the initial CLEARLY in the box. Do not write the whole name, just the first letter.

Now try this

  target C-D

Answer the following questions for the statements above. Who ... ?

(a) enjoys going to the cinema? ☐   **(d)** likes swimming? ☐

(b) likes shopping? ☐   **(e)** goes to the old part of town? ☐

(c) is interested in buildings? ☐

What to do in town

This page gives you lots of useful phrases for describing activities in your town.

In der Stadt

Man kann …	You can …
einen Rundgang machen.	go on a tour.
die Sehenswürdigkeiten besichtigen.	visit the sights.
spazieren gehen.	go for a walk.
den Fluss entlang gehen.	walk along the river.
Fotos machen.	take photos.
Postkarten schicken.	send postcards.
einkaufen gehen.	go shopping.
im Café essen.	eat in a café.
ins Kino gehen.	go to the cinema.
schwimmen gehen.	go swimming.
sich gut amüsieren.	have a good time.
sich mit Freunden treffen.	meet friends.
tanzen gehen.	go dancing.
in den Jugendklub gehen.	go to the youth club.

Negatives

If you want to say what you CAN'T do, use **kein** (not a / no) with an article or **nicht** (not) with a verb.

Man kann **keine** Filme sehen, weil es hier **kein** Kino gibt.
You can't see a film because there is no cinema here.

Hier kann man **nicht** ins Kino gehen, weil es seit einem Jahr geschlossen ist.
You can't go to the cinema here because it has been shut for a year.

Worked example 🎧 36   target B

What is there to do in Karl's town?
A Shopping
B Swimming
C Going to the cinema
Write the correct letter in the box. ☐ B

– Hier, wo ich wohne, gibt es nicht so viel zu tun. Wenn man ins Kino gehen möchte, muss man in die nächste Stadt fahren. Das Gleiche gilt fürs Einkaufen und Restaurants. Im Sommer ist es hier aber OK, weil man ins Freibad gehen und den ganzen Tag im Wasser verbringen kann.

Listening tips

• Listen really CAREFULLY and don't jump to conclusions!

• Use the SECOND LISTENING to double-check you haven't missed anything, such as an important negative.

• Always listen out for NEGATIVES – here **nicht so viel zu tun** (not so much to do).

Karl mentions **Kino** and **Einkaufen**, but don't miss the context for these facilities: **muss man in die nächste Stadt fahren** – you have to go to the **next town** for these facilities.

Now try this 🎧 37   target B

Listen to the rest of Karl's description. Write the correct letter in the box.

1 What does he like about his town?
   A The bowling alley
   B The church
   C His friends ☐

2 What does Karl say about his town?
   A I don't enjoy the excursions with relatives.
   B It's fun going up the church tower.
   C There are lots of interesting sights to visit. ☐

Tourist attractions

You may want to talk about visitor attractions in your speaking assessment. The 24-hour clock is used a lot in German, so check you are confident using it.

Sehenswürdigkeiten

besuchen / besichtigen	to visit
stattfinden	to take place
Auskunft (f)	information
Broschüre (f)	brochure
Touristeninformation (f)	tourist information
Der Eintritt ist €6.	Entry is €6.

Die Rundfahrt beginnt pünktlich um acht Uhr.
The tour begins at eight o'clock prompt.

Der Ausflug findet am Dienstag statt.
The trip takes place on Tuesday.

Es gibt eine Studentenermäßigung.
There is a student discount.

Die Öffnungszeiten sind täglich von neun bis sechzehn Uhr.
The opening times are daily from nine until four o'clock.

Learning vocabulary

- How do you learn vocabulary? Try using learning cards.
- Make your own learning cards – German on one side, English on the other, or a picture on one side, German on the other.
- Use learning cards to help you learn for your assessments. Write key words on them as well as structures you find particularly tricky.

an der Kreuzung links

Worked example

SPEAKING

Was kann man in deiner Stadt machen?

In meiner Stadt gibt es eine gute Kunstgalerie, aber am Montag ist sie geschlossen. Ich gehe oft dahin, weil Kunst mein Lieblingsfach ist.

AIMING HIGHER

Montags kann man leider nicht in die Kunstgalerie gehen, weil sie geschlossen ist, aber sonst kann man sie von 10:00 bis 15:30 Uhr besuchen. Die Ausstellungen dort sind großartig, und die Ermäßigung für Studenten und Senioren ist hervorragend. In den Ferien werde ich im Galeriecafé arbeiten, und so kann ich mir jeden Tag die Bilder kostenlos ansehen kann.

CONTROLLED ASSESSMENT

Students who justify their opinions, use a variety of tenses and, maybe most importantly, develop their answers, do best in the speaking assessments.

Try to add adjectives – the simple addition of **gut** + ending in **eine gute Kunstgalerie** shows you know how to handle German grammar.

Using **großartig** (great) and **hervorragend** (outstanding) makes a refreshing change from the overused **toll**, **klasse** or **super**.

Now try this

SPEAKING

Talk about three things you can do in your town, giving as many details as possible. Talk for about one minute.

- Was kann man in deiner Stadt machen?

Make sure you give any time details correctly using the 24-hour clock and **von ... bis** (from ... until) and include plenty of adjectives to make the places sound like they are worth a visit – **eine Reise wert!**

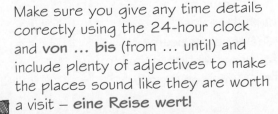

Signs in town

Signs in a town can sometimes be tricky – you need to read them carefully.

Schilder in der Stadt

(Bus)Bahnhof (m)	(bus) station
Abfall / Müll (m)	rubbish
Ausgang (m)	exit
drücken / ziehen	push / pull
Eingang (m)	entrance
Fußgängerzone (f)	pedestrian area
Hauptbahnhof (m)	main station
Sackgasse (f)	no through road
Schnellimbiss (m)	snack bar
Stadtzentrum (n)	town centre
Toiletten (fpl) / WC (n)	toilets
Veranstaltung (f)	event

Notausgang — Emergency exit

Parken verboten — No parking

Herzlich willkommen — Welcome

Negative words

Watch out for these signs which tell you NOT to do something!

nicht	kein	verboten	Achtung	Vorsicht	nicht erlaubt
not	not a / no	forbidden	Attention!	Take care!	Not allowed

Worked example

  target E

What are these signs telling you?

A Schuhe ausziehen

E Abfall in die Tonne werfen

B Rauchen verboten

F Eingang links

C Haustiere sind immer willkommen

G Tür bitte ziehen

D Ausgang rechts

Write the correct letter in the box for question 1.

1 No smoking — B
2 Pull the door — ☐
3 Dogs are welcome — ☐
4 Throw rubbish in the bin — ☐
5 Entrance on the left — ☐

Matching signs

- Look for KEY WORDS in signs like these – Rauchen (smoking) links to question 1 as that is the only one to do with smoking. If you had forgotten what Rauchen was, you can use verboten (forbidden) to lead you to something which is not allowed.

- This reading question has very few words – but you still need to CONCENTRATE to avoid making careless mistakes.

- MATCH the answers you are confident of first. Then go back through the options to see if you can match the others.

Now try this

Complete the activity on the left.

Opinions of your town

When you are writing or speaking about where you live, try to discuss advantages as well as the disadvantages, to include more complex language.

Wie findest du deine Stadt?

Ich wohne gern hier.
I like living here.

Die Stadt hat viel zu bieten.
The town has lots to offer.

Es gibt ein Kino / gute Geschäfte.
There is a cinema / There are good shops.

Es ist eine hübsche Stadt.
It's a pretty town.

Die Stadt ist hässlich und schmutzig.
The town is ugly and dirty.

Heute ist nichts los.
There's nothing going on today.

Ehrlich gesagt, würde ich lieber auf dem Land wohnen.
To be honest, I would prefer to live in the countryside.

Es gibt zu viel Verkehr.
There is too much traffic.

Weil, dass, wo
Grammar page 93

Don't be worried by conjunctions which send the verb to the end – learn a few key phrases to remind you.

Ich wohne nicht gern hier, **weil** es nichts für Teenager **gibt**.
I don't like living here because there is nothing for teenagers.

Es ist ein Vorteil, **dass** ich mit dem Rad in die Schule fahren **kann**.
It is an advantage that I can cycle to school.

Ich würde lieber in einer Stadt wohnen, **wo** es mehr Geschäfte und Klubs **gibt**.
I would prefer to live in a town where there were more shops and clubs.

Worked example

WRITING

Describe where you live.

Ich wohne in einem hässlichen und industriellen Vorort von Genf, wo es nur Gebäude, Fabriken und Büros gibt. Ich würde so gern auf dem Land wohnen, weil die Landschaft dort schön und die Luft frischer ist.

AIMING HIGHER

Als Kind habe ich auf dem Land gewohnt und wir hatten ein riesiges Haus mit einem Garten, der einfach wunderbar war, aber letztes Jahr haben sich meine Eltern scheiden lassen und ich bin mit meiner Mutter nach Berlin umgezogen. Jetzt wohnen wir in einer kleinen Wohnung, aber ich wünsche mir jeden Tag, dass ich wieder auf dem Land wohnen würde.

Aiming higher

1. Make sure you add CONJUNCTIONS to your work, here wo (where) and weil (because).

2. Use a variety of TENSES such as perfect, imperfect, present and conditional.

3. Include GOOD STRUCTURES such as als Kind, haben sich scheiden lassen and ich wünsche mir, dass …

4. Use INTERESTING VOCABULARY such as wunderbar, riesig and winzig.

Now try this

WRITING

Give **three** advantages and **three** disadvantages about where you live.
Write about 100 words in German.

Had a look ☐   Nearly there ☐   Nailed it! ☐

Town description

Giving plenty of facts about your town helps set the scene for a speaking or writing assessment.

Stadtbeschreibung

Einwohner (mpl)	inhabitants
Gegend (f)	area, region
Stadtmitte (f)	town centre
Stadtrand (m)	edge of town
Umgebung (f)	area
Vorort (m)	suburb
Industrie (f)	industry
Landschaft (f)	landscape
Luftverschmutzung (f)	air pollution
50 Kilometer von ... entfernt.	50 km from ...
in der Nähe von	near to
berühmt	famous

North, South, East, West

im Norden

im Westen

im Osten

im Süden

To say NE, NW, SE, SW:

in Südwestengland – in South-west England

in Nordostschottland – in north-east Scotland

Describing your town

* When saying where a town is, offer plenty of information and include adjectives (malerisch, einmalig) and interesting verbs (zählt, liegt, umgeben).

* Look at this high level description for ideas: Knaresborough ist eine malerische Kleinstadt, die ungefähr 15 000 Einwohner zählt. Die Stadt liegt nur 25 Kilometer von Leeds entfernt in Nordengland und ist von einmaliger Landschaft umgeben.

Worked example

Which part of Germany is Dortmund in?

West

– Dortmund ist in Westdeutschland.

Even if you don't hear the full word **Westdeutschland**, you should pick up the 'v' sound of **West-** to help you note the answer.

Check you know what these cities are called in English:

München – Munich   **Köln** – Cologne   **Wien** – Vienna

You won't hear the word **Zentral-** or **Mitte** to indicate a town in the centre of the country, but you will hear **im Herzen** (in the heart), which tells you that this town is in the centre.

Now try this

Listen. Where are these cities: Hamburg, Dresden, Munich and Kassel?

Weather

There are lots of cognates in weather vocabulary, so it shouldn't take you long to master these.

Das Wetter

 Es ist sonnig.   Es ist kalt.   Es ist windig.

 Es ist heiß.   Es ist bewölkt / wolkig.   Es regnet.

 Es donnert und blitzt.   Es ist neblig.   Es schneit.

Es friert.   It's freezing.
Es hagelt.   It's hailing.

Weather in different tenses

Add value to these weather expressions by adapting them to different tenses.

PRESENT Es regnet.   It is raining.

IMPERFECT Es war regnerisch / Es regnete. It was rainy / raining.

PERFECT Es hat geregnet.   It rained.

PLUPERFECT Es hatte geregnet.   It had rained.

FUTURE Es wird regnen.   It will rain.

Try these weather words in different tenses:

Es ist / war / wird ... sein.
It is / was / will be ...

bedeckt	overcast	nass	wet
feucht	damp	sonnig	sunny
heiter	bright	trocken	dry

Worked example   target C

Read the weather forecast.

> Nach Osten hin wird der Wind am Dienstag immer schwächer. Temperaturen liegen bei −14 Grad in den Alpen und bis −1 Grad an der Ostseeküste. Die Nacht über wird es stark schneien. Es bleibt weiterhin bedeckt.

What sort of weather is heading for this area?

A   **B**   **C**

Write the correct letter in the box. ☐ B

EXAM ALERT!

Some students struggle with multiple-choice options as they jump to the wrong conclusion. You must go through each answer option carefully and locate the relevant words in the text to either rule it in or out.

Students have struggled with exam questions similar to this – **be prepared!**

- Read to the very end of the report to find the word **bedeckt** (cloudy), so you can rule out picture C Sunny.
- The minus temperatures and the verb **schneien** (to snow) in the future tense tell you that snow is on its way – answer B.

Now try this   target C

Complete the questions on the text above.

1 The wind ...
  A got stronger yesterday.   **B** will lessen on Tuesday.   **C** will worsen on Tuesday.   ☐

2 The Alpine region will ...
  A be colder than the coast.   **B** be warmer than the coast.   **C** see a lot of rain.   ☐

Celebrations at home

You can include something on celebrations in different writing assessments so learn key phrases.

Zu Hause feiern

Fest (n)	party
Feier (f)	party, celebration
feiern	to celebrate
Feiertag (m)	bank holiday
Feuerwerk (n)	fireworks
Geburtstag (m)	birthday
Geschenk (n)	present
Getränk (n)	drink
zu Hause	at home
Hochzeit (f)	wedding
Nachbarn (mpl)	neighbours
schenken	to give (gift)
sich freuen auf	to look forward to
Fasching	carnival
Ostern	Easter
Silvester	New Year's Eve

Weihnachten
Christmas

Possessive adjectives

 Grammar page 88

These use the same endings as for ein and eine.

Masculine

Ich habe **meinen** Geburtstag gefeiert.
I celebrated my birthday.

Feminine

Ich habe **meine** Geburtstagskarte verloren.
I've lost my birthday card.

Neuter

Ich habe **mein** Geschenk vergessen.
I've forgotten my present.

Plural

Ich habe **meine** Nachbarn eingeladen.
I invited my neighbours.

dein	your	ihr	her / their
sein	your / its	unser	our

Worked example

 LISTENING 40   target B

Thomas is talking about his birthday.
What is his opinion of celebrating it at home?
If positive, write **P**. If negative, write **N**.
If positive and negative, write **P + N**.

☐ N

– Meiner Meinung nach sind Geburtstagsfeste zu Hause kindisch und langweilig. Wenn ich ein Jahr älter werde, will ich bestimmt nicht zu Hause mit meinen Eltern und Geschwistern feiern. Nein, ich gehe viel lieber mit Freunden zum Bowling.

Listening for opinions

- Expressions such as meiner Meinung nach (in my opinion) are obvious pointers to OPINIONS.
- Although somebody might give a negative opinion, one of the answer options is for 'positive and negative', so you have to listen to the ENTIRE PASSAGE to check a positive opinion is not offered as well.
- Listen to the speaker's TONE OF VOICE for any further clues to their opinion.

Now try this

 LISTENING 41   target B

Listen to Nina, Lars and Gabi talking about celebrations at home and complete the above activity for them.

Directions

Have a look at this vocabulary and see if you can direct somebody from your house to the shops.

Richtungen

Gehen Sie ...　Go ... (on foot)

Fahren Sie ...　Drive

 links

 rechts

 geradeaus

 um die Ecke

 über die Brücke

 über den Fluss

 zur Ampel

 an der Kreuzung links

 zum Kreisverkehr

 auf der linken Seite

auf der rechten Seite

Instructions using Sie

Use the Sie form (-en) of the verb + Sie:

Überqueren Sie die Straße.

Cross the road.

Gehen Sie an der Ampel rechts.
Go right at the lights.

Instructions using du

Grammar page 97

For gehen and other regular present tense verbs use the du form minus the final -st:

Geh die Einbahnstraße hinunter.

Go down the one-way street.

Use fahr for fahren: Fahr Richtung München.

Drive in the direction of Munich.

Worked example

 LISTENING 42　 target C

Listen. How do you get to the market place?

A Left, then over the crossroads.

B Left, then over the bridge.

C Right, then round the corner.

Write the correct letter in the box.　B

– Zum Marktplatz gehen Sie hier gleich links und dann gehen Sie 100 Meter geradeaus. Sie kommen dann zum Fluss, wo es eine Fußgängerbrücke gibt. Gehen Sie hinüber und Sie sehen den Marktplatz auf der rechten Seite.

- **Say** these directions to yourself in German before you play the recording.

- Make sure you get **rechts** or **links** correct, as both are mentioned by the speaker. You need **links** here as that is the first direction given.

- **Fluss** (river), **Fußgängerbrücke** (footbridge) and **hinüber** (over) are the clues to lead you to answer B, over the bridge.

Now try this

 SPEAKING

Prepare 4–6 sentences in German to give instructions for directions A and C above.

At the train station

You may meet station vocabulary in listening and reading texts, so it's well worth learning it.

Am Bahnhof

Abfahrt (f)	departure
Ankunft (f)	arrival
aussteigen	to get off
den Zug verpassen	to miss the train
einsteigen	to get on
entwerten	to punch a ticket
Fahrer (m)	driver
Fahrkartenautomat (m)	ticket machine
Fahrkartenschalter (m)	ticket counter
Fahrschein (m)	ticket
Gepäckaufbewahrung (f)	left luggage
Gleis (n)	platform
Karte (f)	ticket
Rückfahrkarte (f)	return ticket
Schlafwagen (m)	sleeping carriage
Verspätung haben	to be delayed
Wartesaal (m)	waiting room
Zuschlag (m)	supplement

24-hour clock

The 24-hour clock – easy if you know your numbers!

It is used for opening times, train times or to say when an event is taking place.

 **09:30** neun Uhr dreißig

 **12:45** zwölf Uhr fünfundvierzig

 **16:15** sechzehn Uhr fünfzehn

 **20:40** zwanzig Uhr vierzig

 **23:00** dreiundzwanzig Uhr

Add the word **Uhr** between the hour and the minutes to show 'o'clock'.

um – at: **um zwanzig Uhr** (at 20.00 hours).

  Worked example LISTENING 43 | target D

Listen and answer the questions.

(a) What time is the passenger catching the train? 7.30

(b) What time will the passenger arrive? 8.40

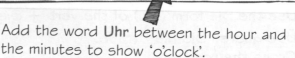

– Also, Sie möchten nach Bremen fahren. Der nächste Zug fährt um sieben Uhr dreißig ab. Sie kommen dann um acht Uhr vierzig in Bremen an.

EXAM ALERT!

Students who write the numbers unclearly or in tiny illegible writing often don't do so well as it is difficult to decide whether the answer is correct or not. Make sure that you write numbers (and letters) clearly and properly in the spaces provided.

Students have struggled with exam questions similar to this – **be prepared!**

- Don't make careless mistakes by confusing **vierzig** (40) with **vierzehn** (14), etc.

- Listen carefully for separable verbs like **abfahren** – **ab** might have split from **fahren**, so listen to the whole sentence to check the time relates to a departure time, not an arrival.

Focus on the departure and arrival times **only** – you can ignore any other information, as it is not needed to answer the questions.

  Now try this LISTENING 44 | target D

Listen to **three** more travel arrangements. Answer the above questions for these passengers.

- Departure time?
- Arrival time?

Travelling

Don't forget the Time – Manner – Place rule when you are saying how you travel somewhere.

Verkehrsmittel

mit dem Auto / Wagen

mit der Bahn / mit dem Zug

mit dem Boot / Schiff

mit dem Bus

mit dem Rad (Fahrrad)

mit dem Flugzeug

mit dem Mofa

mit dem Motorrad

mit der Straßenbahn   zu Fuß

DB = Deutsche Bahn
ICE = Intercity-Express

Time – Manner – Place

A detail of transport counts as Manner, so put it AFTER a Time expression, but BEFORE a Place. **Grammar page 92**

T   gestern / heute / letzte Woche / in der Zukunft

M   mit dem Zug / zu Fuß / mit meiner Familie

P   nach London / in die Stadt / über die Brücke

Ich bin letzte Woche mit der Straßenbahn gefahren.

Ich fahre heute mit der U-Bahn in die Stadtmitte.

Worked example   SPEAKING

Wie kommst du in die Stadt?

Ich finde, dass die U-Bahn praktisch und zuverlässig ist, obwohl manchmal zu viele Leute unterwegs sind.

Giving an opinion with **Ich denke / finde, dass** … raises the level of your speaking, as does using subordinating conjunctions such as **obwohl** (although).

AIMING HIGHER   Ich muss nie länger als fünf Minuten warten und jeder Zug kommt pünktlich an. Wenn unsere öffentlichen Verkehrsmittel nicht so effizient wären, würden viele Leute noch mit dem Auto fahren und das würde ich schade finden.

- This student has added a **modal verb** and used a **comparative adjective** to show a confident command of the German language.
- The inclusion of a **wenn** phrase coupled with the idiom **es schade finden** (to find it a shame) really helps this student to aim higher.

Now try this   SPEAKING

Answer the questions with as much detail as possible. Talk for about **one** minute in German.

- Wie fährst du in die Stadt? Warum?
- Wie fährst du in Urlaub? Warum?

Transport

You may well meet transport vocabulary in a reading text. Watch out for words like nie (never), jeder (every) and trotz (despite). They can be crucial for meaning.

Verkehrsmittel

Autobahn (f)	motorway
Benzin (n)	petrol
bleifrei	lead free
Fahrpreis (m)	fare
Fahrradweg (m)	cycle path
Fahrt (f)	journey
Motor (m)	engine
öffentliche Verkehrsmittel (npl)	public transport
Passagier (m)	passenger
Stau (m)	traffic jam
Tankstelle (f)	petrol station
Verkehr (m)	traffic
Verschmutzung (f)	pollution

Opinions

Use Ich glaube, dass (I believe that) or Ich finde, dass (I think that) as handy ways to add an opinion. Dass sends the verb to the end of the clause.

Fahrradwege sind ausgezeichnet. Cycle paths are excellent. ➡

Ich finde, dass Fahrradwege ausgezeichnet sind.
I think that cycle paths are great.

Here are some other adjectives you could use when talking about transport:

bequem	comfortable
praktisch	practical
pünktlich	punctual
schädlich	harmful
umweltfreundlich	environmentally friendly

Worked example

Read Hanna's blog about transport.

> Ich denke, dass jeder versuchen sollte, so oft wie möglich mit der Bahn zu fahren, weil die Benzinpreise immer mehr steigen und die Autoabgase zu einer unakzeptablen Luftverschmutzung führen.

Why does Hanna think people should travel by train more? Give **two** reasons.

1 Higher petrol prices
2 Unacceptable levels of air pollution from cars

- The **first** part of the sentence tells you that Hanna thinks people should travel by train more – so it is the **next** part that will provide your answer.
- Make sure you answer **in English** – there is no point in writing out any German words from the text. If you really can't work out the meaning of the word, you will have to make an **intelligent guess**, which is better than leaving the space blank.

Now try this

Read the text and answer the questions below in English.

(a) How does Shayden find the public transport system in Munich compared with that in England?

(b) What would make it better in England?

Shayden aus Coventry

Ich bin Fremdsprachenassistent in München. Ich finde es total fantastisch, wie viel besser die öffentlichen Verkehrsmittel hier in München sind als in meiner Heimatstadt in England. Wenn unser Staat mehr Geld in Busse und die Bahn investieren würde, hätten wir vielleicht auch ein wunderbares öffentliches Transportsystem. Wir hätten auch eine bessere Luftqualität für alle Einwohner.

The environment

Look at the strategies on this page to help you tackle higher reading texts.

Die Umwelt

Abgase (npl)	emissions
Benzin (n)	petrol
Brennstoff (m)	fuel
heizen	to heat
Kohle (f)	coal
Öltanker (m)	oil tanker
Ozonloch (n)	hole in the ozone layer
Sauerstoff (m)	oxygen
schaden	to damage
schützen	to protect
schädlich	harmful
Treibhauseffekt (m)	greenhouse effect
Treibhausgas (n)	greenhouse gas
Verschmutzung (f)	pollution
verschwinden	to disappear
zerstören	to destroy

Adverbs

Adverbs are the same as adjectives in German.

Adjective

Das ist schnell.	That is quick.

Adverb

Mach das schnell.	Do that quickly.
erwartungsvoll	expectantly
glücklich	happily
(un)geduldig	(im)patiently

Die Abgase in der Stadt sind gefährlich.

Worked example

Read a blog entry about the environment.

Warum machen wir unsere Erde kaputt?
Wir wollen die Erde schützen statt ihr zu schaden, aber wir sind nicht bereit, mit dem Bus statt mit dem Auto zum Einkaufen zu fahren. Wir suchen immer nach Alternativen, unsere Häuser zu heizen, aber die Öltanker überqueren immer noch den Ozean, um uns diesen Brennstoff zu bringen. Wir hoffen auf natürliche Energiequellen, aber es kostet Geld, sie zu entwickeln, und da wir keine gute Lösung finden, wird das Ozonloch immer größer. Wir machen uns Sorgen über die Wasserverschmutzung sowie die Luftverschmutzung in unseren Städten, aber wir tun wenig dagegen …

Read this statement about the blog.

Write **T** if it is true. Write **F** if it is false.

Write **?** if it is not in the text.

We want to protect our planet.   T

Strategies for unknown words

- Break longer words down: Wasser (water) + Verschmutzung (pollution).
- Use other German words: Lösung is difficult, but you might know lösen (to solve), so you can work out that Lösung = solution.
- Use English cognates: Alternativen (alternatives).
- Use the question and context: the statement on the text mentions 'protect' – that gives you a context to identify the German for 'protect' and work out the answer.

Now try this

Complete the above activity for these sentences. True, false, or not in the text?

(a) People's means of transport have changed.

(b) Transporting fuel is expensive.

(c) Water pollution is no longer an issue.

(d) You can donate money to help combat air pollution.

Environmental issues

Try to include an **als** sentence when talking about environmental issues to show good command of German word order in the past tense.

Umweltprobleme

Gefahr (f)	danger
Lärm (m)	noise
bedrohen	to threaten
den Müll trennen	to separate rubbish
im Stau sitzen	to sit in a traffic jam
produzieren	to produce
verschmutzen	to pollute
gefährlich	dangerous

mit den öffentlichen Verkehrsmitteln fahren
to go by public transport

Abfalleimer (m) /
Mülltonne (f)

Radweg (m)

Verkehr (m)

Verpackung (f)

Using als

- Use **als** to mean 'when' in the past tense.

  Note that it sends the verb to the end, then a comma followed by the next verb.

  Als ich nach Hamburg fuhr, war der Verkehr schrecklich.
  When I drove to Hamburg, the traffic was awful.

- But use **wenn** to mean 'when' in the present tense.

  Wenn ich mit den öffentlichen Verkehrsmitteln fahre, helfe ich der Umwelt.
  When I use public transport, I help the environment.

Worked example

 LISTENING 45   target A-A*

Listen and answer the question **in English**.
What **two** things does Kai consider a problem in his town?

1 People throw rubbish on the ground.
2 We use too much packaging.

– Meinst du, dass es in deiner Stadt Umweltprobleme gibt?

– Ja, sicher. Obwohl wir alle zu Hause den Müll trennen, passiert es oft in der Stadt, dass man den Abfall immer noch auf den Boden wirft. Ich finde es auch schade, dass immer noch Produkte mit zu viel bunter Verpackung verkauft werden. Das finde ich unnötig.

EXAM ALERT!

At the end of the higher listening paper, you have questions to answer in English. Some students find this challenging. If **two** details are asked for (usually given in bold print), you need to supply **two** details. Always read the questions carefully before you listen, so you know exactly what you're listening for.

> Students have struggled with exam questions similar to this – **be prepared!**

Now try this

 LISTENING 46   target A-A*

Listen to the rest of Kai's interview and to an interview with Sophie. Answer the questions in English.

(a) What other example does Kai give for the problem he mentions?
(b) What is the main problem according to Sophie?
(c) What are the consequences of this problem? Give **two** details.
(d) What does Sophie think would help the problem? Give **three** details.

What I do to be 'green'

Talk about how you help the environment, not just regularly, but what you did in the past and what you will do in the future too if you are aiming for a higher grade.

Wie ich der Umwelt helfe

Ich fahre mit den öffentlichen Verkehrsmitteln.
I travel by public transport.
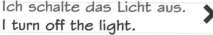

Ich schalte das Licht aus.
I turn off the light.

Ich benutze nie Spraydosen.
I never use aerosols.

Ich gehe sparsam mit der Zentralheizung um.
I am economical with the central heating.

Ich kaufe Pfandflaschen.
I buy bottles with a deposit.

sammeln	to collect
sparen	to save
wegwerfen	to throw away
umweltfreundlich	eco-friendly

The ich form

You are most likely to talk about what you do using the ich form.

PRESENT: Ich recycle Kleidung.
I recycle clothes.

PAST: Ich habe Kleidung recycelt.
I recycled clothes.

IMPERFECT: Ich recycelte Kleidung.
I used to recycle clothes.

FUTURE: Ich werde Kleidung recyceln.
I will recycle clothes.

Ich trenne den Müll.

Worked example

LISTENING 47   target D

Herr Eiger is providing information about recycling facilities at school.

What can be recycled?

A   B   C   D

Write the correct letters in the boxes.   B C

– Herr Eiger, was kann man hier in der Schule recyceln?

– Hier in der Schule recyceln wir viel. In jedem Klassenzimmer gibt es eine Mülltonne für Altpapier und in der Kantine sammelt man Biomüll. Man wirft keine Speisereste weg.

Exam strategies

- Always read the QUESTION first – here you need to identify items that CAN be recycled.
- Look at the KIND of answer you need to give – here there are two empty boxes and you need to put a letter A–D in each box.
- INTELLIGENT GUESSWORK is a good idea – wild guesses are not. Use the words you have understood to come up with a plausible answer. Here, you might not understand Biomüll (food waste) but you should recognise Kantine, which can lead you to the correct answer.

Now try this

LISTENING 48   target D

Listen to the rest of the interview. How else does the school help the environment?

A It provides its own solar energy.
B It is fitting eight solar panels on the roof.
C It helps the environment now and again.
D It is extremely environmentally friendly.

Write the **two** correct letters in the boxes.   ☐ ☐

Had a look ☐ Nearly there ☐ Nailed it! ☐

News headlines

Look at the news headlines on a German internet site from time to time. You may be surprised at what you can understand!

Die Schlagzeilen

im Ausland	abroad
Gefahr (f)	danger
Gewalttätigkeit (f)	violence
Schutz (m)	protection
Straftat (f)	crime
Sturm (m)	storm
Unfall (m)	accident
Hungersnot (f)	famine
Krankheit (f)	disease
sich ärgern	to be angry / upset
sich entscheiden	to decide
leiden	to suffer
spenden	to donate money
verletzt	injured
weltweit	worldwide

Reflexive verbs (accusative)

Grammar page 96

Ich interessiere mich für die Nachrichten.
I am interested in the news.

Ich ärgere mich darüber.
I am angry about it.

Er / sie + sich: Er freut sich (auf) …
He's looking forward (to) …

du + dich: Freust du dich darauf?

wir + uns: Wir freuen uns darauf.

Sie + sich: Sie freuen sich darauf.

Schwere Schäden und Verletzte im ersten Herbststurm.
Serious problems and injuries in the first storm of Autumn.

Worked example

 READING   target B

You read the news headlines.

Aktivisten berichten von Gefahr im Militärhauptquartier. Eine Bombe explodierte und auf beiden Seiten gab es ☐ Soldaten. Man ist dabei, die Familien zu informieren und die Verstorbenen nach Hause zu bringen.

Write the letter of the missing word in the box. ☐ A

A tote **B** keine **C** verletzte

EXAM ALERT!

Students who do well in this type of task are the ones who read all the text before they choose their answer option. Sometimes you might think the answer is obvious if you only read a few words before the gap, but if you read the whole text, you might discover the word you thought filled the gap, actually does not.

Students have struggled with exam questions similar to this – **be prepared!**

Now try this

 READING   target B

Which word fills the gap? Write the correct letter in the box.

1 Der Generalstreik in Griechenland hält an. Busfahrer, Lehrer und Beamte haben alle den ☐ verlassen. Millionen von Menschen wollen damit gegen das neue Sparprogramm protestieren.

A Stadtrand **B** Unfall **C** Arbeitsplatz ☐

2 In Ostafrika wird die Situation schlimmer statt besser. Tausende Menschen von ☐ sind bedroht. Epidemien bedrohen eine Generation von kleinen Kindern, die nicht genug zu essen bekommen. Noch nie ist die Arbeit der Hilfsorganisationen so notwendig gewesen …

A Wasserverschmutzung **B** Hungersnot
C Gewalttätigkeit ☐

School subjects

Knowledge of school subject vocabulary is useful for listening and reading assessments.

Schulfächer

 Mathe(matik)
 Biologie
 Chemie

 Physik
 Deutsch
 Englisch

 Französisch
 Spanisch
 Erdkunde

 Geschichte
 Religion
 Informatik

 Kunst
Sport

seit + present tense

To talk about how long you have been doing something, use seit + present tense.

Ich lerne seit vier Jahren Deutsch.
I have been learning German for four years.

The noun after seit (since) needs to be in the DATIVE case.

seit vier Monaten
for four months

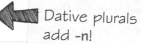 Dative plurals add -n!

seit diesem Semester	since this semester
seit letztem Jahr	since last year
seit letzter Woche	since last week

Seit drei Jahren lerne ich Japanisch.

Pflichtfach (n)	compulsory subject	Medienwissenschaft (f)	media studies
Wahlfach (n)	optional subject	schwach / stark	weak / strong
Kochen (n)	cookery	Theater (n)	drama
		Werken (n)	design and technology

Worked example

LISTENING 48   target C

Birk is talking about his new school.
Why does he like Thursdays?

He has double art / likes the art teacher.

– Ich mag meine Schule. Mein Lieblingstag ist Donnerstag, weil ich dann eine Doppelstunde Kunst habe und die Lehrerin sehr sympathisch ist.

Answering questions in English

- Make sure your answers are concise and that they really DO answer the question.
- English questions normally only need 3–4 word answers, so do not write down EVERYTHING you hear.
- Do not write GERMAN words down – they will not be marked.
- Sometimes you will hear more than one answer option to write down – here, you could have either 'He has double art' or 'He likes the art teacher'.

Now try this

LISTENING 49   target C

Listen. What does Birk find negative and positive about the school? Give one for each.

1 Negative: _____

2 Positive: _____

Opinions about school

You need to give lots of opinions – with reasons – if you are aiming for a higher grade.

Meinungen über die Schule

Meiner Meinung nach ist Chemie einfach.
In my opinion chemistry is easy.

Ich finde, dass Mathe schwierig ist.
I think that maths is difficult.

Es ist gut, dass die Schule so erfolgreich ist.
It is good that the school is so successful.

Die Regeln sind (un)fair / dumm / blöd.
The rules are (un)fair / stupid.

Die Lehrer sind streng / mies.
The teachers are strict / horrible.

Man bekommt zu viele Hausaufgaben.
You get too much homework.

Ich habe immer Angst vor den Noten.
I am always afraid of the grades.

Mein Lieblingsfach ist Werken.
My favourite subject is DT.

Fillers

Use fillers to make you sound more fluent.

absolut — absolutely
bestimmt — certainly
wirklich — really
doch — yet, but, however
sicher — certainly
Fillers

Ich finde Deutsch wirklich super.
I find German really great.

Spanisch ist bestimmt schwierig.
Spanish is certainly difficult.

Worked example 🗣 SPEAKING

Wie findest du die Schule?

Meiner Meinung nach ist Mathe sehr schwierig, besonders wenn man kein fleißiger Schüler ist. Ich finde Sport viel besser, weil wir nie Klassenarbeiten schreiben müssen.

AIMING HIGHER

Es ist absolut fair, dass Rauchen auf dem Schulgelände streng verboten ist, weil Rauchen sowieso schlecht für die Gesundheit ist. Die Schule kann aber stressig sein. Wenn ich schlechte Noten bekomme, habe ich auch ein schlechtes Zeugnis. Dann werden meine Eltern sicher böse sein. In der Grundschule hatte man weder Prüfungen noch Stress, und dafür hatte man den ganzen Tag lang nur Spaß!

This student offers a couple of **opinions** and uses a **modal** with a conjunction, but it is all in the **present** tense.

This student uses a variety of elements and structures to give her opinion:

- fillers: **absolut**, **sicher**
- present, future and past tenses
- modal verb
- **dass**, **weil** and **wenn** clauses + correct word order.

German school grades

1 = sehr gut, 2 = gut, 3 = befriedigend (satisfactory), 4 = ausreichend (adequate), 5 = mangelhaft (unsatisfactory), 6 = ungenügend (inadequate).

Now try this 🗣 SPEAKING

Answer these questions about your school in German.

- Was ist dein Lieblingsfach? Warum?
- Findest du diese Schule besser als die Grundschule? Warum?
- Was magst du / magst du nicht besonders an deiner Schule? Warum?
- Und was magst du nicht? Warum?

Always give your opinion **and** the reason for that opinion.

School routine

School routine is often chosen as a topic for the speaking or writing assessment, so make sure you can say something a bit unusual to stand out from the crowd.

Der Schultag

Der Schultag beginnt um zehn vor neun.
The school day starts at ten to nine.
Wir haben sechs Stunden pro Tag.
We have six lessons each day.
Jeden Morgen gibt es eine Versammlung.
There is an assembly each morning.
In der Pause gehen wir auf den Schulhof.
At break we go to the playground.
Wir essen zu Mittag in der Kantine.
We eat lunch in the canteen.
Man kann in der Bibliothek Hausaufgaben machen.
You can do homework in the library.
Nach der Schule gibt es eine gute Auswahl an AGs.
After school there is a good selection of clubs.
Sport haben wir immer als Doppelstunde.
We always have a double lesson for PE.

Linking words

Grammar page 93

These make your sentences longer and DON'T change the word order!

aber but   oder or
denn because   und   and

In der Pause plaudern wir oder wir machen Hausaufgaben.
At break we chat or do homework.

Worked example  *target C*

Read the text.

> Um sechs Uhr wache ich auf, denn der Wecker klingelt und ich muss zur Schule gehen. Ich würde natürlich lieber noch im warmen Bett bleiben, aber das geht leider nicht.

Write the correct letter in the box. ☐ B

A Beth wakes up at 7 o'clock.
B Beth is reluctant to get up.
C Beth's mum wakes her up.

Sometimes you have to **infer** meaning. Beth doesn't say explicitly 'I don't like getting up', but the fact that she **would prefer** to stay in the warm bed tells you she is 'reluctant to get up'.

Reading tips

- In this style of activity, the accompanying statements will always be in the SAME ORDER as the text.
- Cross through any statements that are wrong. Here, Beth wakes up at 6 o'clock, so sentence A is clearly wrong.

Now try this *target C*

Now read the rest of the passage. What does Beth say about her school routine?

S-Bahn – local train

> Schule ist Pflicht! Ich muss hin! Nach dem Frühstück fahre ich mit der S-Bahn zur Schule. Die Fahrt dauert eine halbe Stunde und unterwegs mache ich meine Hausaufgaben. Die Schule beginnt pünktlich um zehn nach acht und ich muss im Klassenzimmer sein, sonst bekomme ich eine Strafarbeit. Als Erstes habe ich heute eine Doppelstunde Chemie – mein Lieblingsfach ist das nicht! Ich freue mich aber auf die dritte Stunde, weil das Sport ist!

A Beth goes to school by tram.
B Beth does homework on the journey.

C Beth has to be in class at ten past eight.
D Beth likes chemistry.

Write the **two** correct letters in the boxes. ☐ ☐

German schools

If you write about schools in your assessment, you could make comparisons with German schools.

Deutsche Schulen

Direktor (m) / Direktorin (f)	headteacher
Schulleiter (m) / Schulleiterin (f)	headteacher
in die Schule gehen	to attend school
studieren	to study
unterrichten	to teach
Berufsschule (f)	vocational school
Gesamtschule (f)	comprehensive school
Grundschule (f)	primary school
Gymnasium (n)	grammar school
Hauptschule / Realschule (f)	type of secondary school
Kindergarten (m)	pre-school
Internat (n)	boarding school
Zeugnis (n)	report

Using müssen (to have to) — Grammar page 98

Müssen is a modal verb so it needs an infinitive at the end of the sentence.

Man muss Hausaufgaben machen.
You have to do homework.

Man muss … / You have to …	höflich sein. be polite.
	viel üben, um ein Instrument zu spielen. practise a lot to play an instrument.
	sitzen bleiben. repeat a school year.

Man muss rechtzeitig zur Schule kommen.
You have to get to school on time.

Worked example

Write about your school experience.

Ich gehe auf ein gemischtes Gymnasium. Meine Schule ist sehr modern. Sie wurde zweitausendzehn geöffnet. Wir haben viele Computer im Klassenzimmer.

AIMING HIGHER

Ich gehe auf eine Gesamtschule, die etwa tausend Schüler und Schülerinnen hat. Als ich in die siebte Klasse kam, war ich sehr nervös, weil das Schulgebäude einfach so groß war. In der elften Klasse bin ich jetzt viel selbstbewusster und ich fange an, mich richtig auf die Oberstufe zu freuen. Hoffentlich werde ich nicht bei den Prüfungen durchfallen.

CONTROLLED ASSESSMENT

Students aiming for a higher grade need to show a consistent use of correct word order. This includes placing the verb second in the sentence, using the Time, Manner, Place rule and including a range of subordinating conjunctions + verb to the end, such as **weil**, **wenn**, **obwohl**.

Extra features here aiming higher are:
- relative pronoun, **eine Gesamtschule, die**
- opinion + **weil** + **als** clause
- comparative, **selbstbewusster**
- **ich fange an** + **zu** + infinitive construction
- **hoffentlich** + future tense.

Now try this

Write a paragraph in German, of about 100 words, to describe your school, using the examples above to help you.

Primary school

Talking about your primary school provides a great opportunity to use the imperfect tense.

Die Grundschule

In der Grundschule …
At primary school …
  durfte man draußen essen.
  you were allowed to eat outside.
  musste man keine Hausaufgaben machen
  you didn't have to do homework.
  hatte ich viele Freunde.
  I had a lot of friends.
  gab es keinen Stress.
  there wasn't any stress.
  waren die Lehrer nett.
  the teachers were nice.

> Grammar page 99

Modals – imperfect tense

kann – can	➡	konnte – could
muss – have to	➡	musste – had to
darf – am allowed	➡	durfte – was allowed
will – want	➡	wollte – wanted
soll – shall	➡	sollte – should
mag – like	➡	mochte – liked

In der Grundschule … At primary school …	konnte ich kein Französisch sprechen. I couldn't speak French. musste meine Mutter mich zur Schule bringen. my mum had to take me to school.

der Bleistift   die Federmappe   der Filzstift

der Klebstoff   der Kuli   das Lineal   der Radiergummi   der Taschenrechner

Worked example

READING · target A

Read the text.

In der Grundschule habe ich mich immer gut benommen, aber mein Bruder Tim wollte nie das machen, was er sollte. Mein Vater bat ihn sehr oft, mehr im Haushalt zu helfen, aber Tim blieb mit Kopfhörern in seinem Zimmer und hörte ihm nicht zu. Meine Eltern sagten Tim, dass er mehr wie ich sein sollte. Wenn ich etwas Dummes machte, lachte mein Vater, aber mit Tim war er immer böse.

When Tim was younger …
A he was not very obedient at school.
B he was a well-behaved pupil.
C he always got good marks.
Write the correct letter in the box. ☐A☐

EXAM ALERT!

For this task, good comprehension skills are needed, as well as an ability to draw conclusions from the text. The questions are not phrased in exactly the same way as they appear in the text, so be careful!

> Students have struggled with exam questions similar to this – **be prepared!**

Now try this

READING · target A

Complete the sentences. Write the correct letter in the box.

1 Tim …
  A ignored his father.   B was occasionally asked to help out.   C suffered from headaches. ☐
2 Their dad reacted to both of them …
  A proudly.   B in the same way.   C in different ways. ☐

Rules at school

When talking about your school, you may want to say what you like and don't like, as well as what the rules are. Learn some of these phrases.

Schulregeln

Mit achtzehn Jahren darf man die Schule verlassen.
You can leave school at 18.

Die Regeln finde ich (un)gerecht.
I find the rules (un)fair.

Man darf das Handy im Klassenzimmer nicht benutzen.
You are not allowed to use your phone in class.

Man darf nicht zu spät in die Schule kommen.
You are not allowed to arrive late at school.

Im Schulgebäude darf man keinen Kaugummi kauen.
You can't eat gum in the school building.

Man darf bei Prüfungen nicht abschreiben.
You are not allowed to copy in exams.

Man muss nachsitzen.
You get detention.

Viele Schüler machen blau / schwänzen.
A lot of students play truant.

Obwohl

Grammar page 93

Obwohl (although) is a subordinating conjunction which sends the verb to the end of the clause, like weil.

Obwohl es eine kleine Schule ist, gibt es hier viele AGs.
Although it is a small school, there are lots of clubs here.

Er ist zur Schule gegangen, obwohl er schreckliche Kopfschmerzen hatte.
He went to school, although he had a terrible headache.

Worked example

  target D

Read these signs at school.

A Kaugummi im Klassenzimmer verboten!
B Zu spät zur Schule? Geh direkt zum Lehrerzimmer.
C Hausaufgaben nie vergessen.
D Ruhe bitte! Prüfung findet statt.
E *Handys müssen in der Schultasche bleiben.*
F Die Schulregeln sind im Sekretariat zu lesen.

Which sign matches this person?

Write the correct letter in the box.

Ralf has to go to the staff room. ☐ B

EXAM ALERT!

- Use black ink for your answers and press clearly with the pen.
- Answer only in the space provided.
- All listening and reading papers are marked onscreen and faint marks might not be picked up.
- Do not make assumptions – you need to read every word in tasks like this where there is not much text. It might be the smallest of words that holds the answer.

Students have struggled with exam questions similar to this – **be prepared!**

Now try this

  target D

Which sign matches which person? Write the correct letters in the boxes.

1 There is an exam on. ☐
2 Teresa is looking for the school rules. ☐
3 No chewing gum. ☐
4 Keep your mobile phone in your bag. ☐

There are always more signs, texts or pictures than people to match them to, but read **each** of them in order to discount the ones you **don't need**.

School problems

Talking about school problems and issues can help you to aim higher in the speaking and writing assessments.

Schulprobleme

Im Klassenzimmer ist es laut und unangenehm.
It is loud and unpleasant in the classroom.

Ich finde die Lehrer zu streng.
I find the teachers too strict.

Viele Schüler leiden unter Schulstress.
Many students suffer from stress at school.

Es gibt zu viel Leistungsdruck.
There is too much pressure to achieve.

Ich habe Angst vor der Abschlussprüfung.
I am afraid of the final exams.

Die Prüfungsergebnisse sind am wichtigsten.
The exam results are the most important.

Ich bekomme oft / nie Strafarbeiten.
I often / never get punishments.

Using man

- Use man to mean one / you / somebody / people.
- Man takes the er / sie part of the verb.

Present tense

Man muss zur Schule gehen.
You have to go to school.

Future tense

Man wird das verbessern.
One will improve that.

Don't confuse with der Mann – the man.

Als Schüler hat man zu viele Prüfungen.

Worked example

Complete the text with **one** of the words that follow. Write the correct letter in the box.

> Ich bin total gestresst, weil ich die Physikhausaufgaben gar nicht verstehe und wir gleich nach der Pause ▯ mit Frau Thomas haben.

A Mathe   **B** verstehen
C Naturwissenschaften   C

Tips for gapped statements

- Read the WHOLE of the text with the gap and try to understand the gist of it.
- Then decide what SORT OF WORD fits into the gap. This will help to reduce your choices.
- Make WORD CONNECTIONS – here, Physik (physics) and Naturwissenschaften (sciences) are linked.

Now try this

Complete these texts with **one** of the words that follow. Write the correct letters in the boxes.

1 An der Schule leidet man oft an ▯▯▯ , weil die Lehrer, die Eltern und die Schüler es so wichtig finden, immer gute Noten zu bekommen.

2 Meine Eltern wären sehr enttäuscht, wenn ich die ▯▯▯ am Ende des Schuljahres nicht bestehe.

3 Wenn man nicht den Regeln folgt, bekommt man Ärger von den Lehrern. Das Schlimmste ist, wenn man zum ▯▯▯ gehen muss.

4 Wenn man den Schulstress ▯▯▯ will, könnte man Sport treiben oder im Orchester spielen. Das ist entspannend.

A Abschlussprüfung   **C** Direktor   **E** Hause
B verzeihen   **D** Leistungsdruck   **F** bewältigen

Future education plans

Talking about future plans enables you to say what you WANT to do over the next few years.

Zukunftspläne

Ich möchte / werde …	I would like to / will …
das Jahr wiederholen.	repeat the year.
die Schule verlassen.	leave school.
eine Prüfung bestehen.	pass an exam.
einen Studienplatz bekommen.	get a college place.
eine Ausbildung machen.	do training.
Arbeitserfahrung suchen.	look for work experience.

Berufsberater (m)	careers adviser
Berufsschule (f)	vocational college
Resultat / Ergebnis (n)	result
Mittlere Reife (f)	GCSE equivalent
Abitur (Abi) (n)	A-level equivalent
Abiturient/in (m/f)	student with Abitur
Abschlusszeugnis (n)	leaving certificate
Qualifikation (f)	qualification
Student/in (m/f)	student

Using wollen

Grammar page 98

Wollen (to want) is a modal verb, so it needs an infinitive.

Ich will auf die Oberstufe gehen.
I want to go into the sixth form.

Don't confuse the German **will** with the English 'will' (future intent). It means 'want to do something'.

Ich will … I want to …	… weiterstudieren. … carry on studying.
	… auf die Universität (Uni) gehen. … go to uni.
	… eine Lehre machen. …do an apprenticeship.

Ich will Englisch und Geschichte an der Uni studieren.

Worked example

Was wirst du nach der Mittleren Reife machen?

Gleich nach den Prüfungen will ich ein Wochenende mit meiner Clique an der Küste verbringen. Ich freue mich irrsinnig darauf, obwohl meine Eltern nicht so begeistert darüber sind. Nächstes Jahr werde ich hoffentlich in die Oberstufe kommen, wenn ich die notwendigen Noten bekomme. Ich will Fremdsprachen und Mathe studieren, weil ich eines Tages gern im Ausland arbeiten möchte.

Speaking tips

- If you speak quickly because you are nervous, try to SLOW yourself DOWN so you make the minimum time of 4 minutes.

- Play for time if your mind goes blank by asking Wie bitte? Or REPEAT part of the question in your answer.

- You will be asked ONE unpredictable question. The more you have prepared in advance on your chosen topic, the more confident you will be to tackle anything you are asked.

Now try this

Prepare 4–6 sentences in German in answer to the following question.
- Was wirst du nach der Mittleren Reife machen?

Record yourself and listen back to hear how German you sound. Good pronunciation and intonation show you are aiming higher.

Future careers

Use the expressions on this page to include some high level language when you are talking about your future career.

Die berufliche Zukunft

Ich hoffe, ... I hope ...

für eine große Firma zu arbeiten.
to work for a large company.

einen hohen Lohn zu verdienen.
to earn a high wage.

nicht in einer Fabrik zu arbeiten.
not to work in a factory.

(nicht) draußen / im Freien zu arbeiten.
(not) to work outside.

ganztags zu arbeiten.
to work full time.

eine Teilzeitarbeit zu finden.
to find a part-time job.

von zu Hause zu arbeiten.
to work from home.

mit sympathischen Kollegen zusammen zu arbeiten.
to work with nice colleagues.

Infinitive expressions

 Grammar page 94

Ich ...	hoffe, ... (hope)	+ zu + infinitive.
	versuche, ... (try)	
	habe vor, ... (intend)	

Ich habe vor, ins Ausland zu reisen.
I intend to travel abroad.

Ich hoffe, viel Geld zu verdienen.
I hope to earn lots of money.

Ich versuche, einen Nebenjob zu finden.
I am trying to find a part-time job.

Worked example   LISTENING 50 target C

Florian is giving his opinion on his new job.

What does Florian say is the advantage of his job?

A He has an annoying boss.
B He has a young boss.
C He often does shift work.
D It is a big company.
E He lives nearby.

Write the correct letter in the box. ☐ E

– Ich arbeite bei einer großen Autofirma in München. Ich wohne ganz in der Nähe und es gibt einen Radweg von meinem Wohnblock bis zur Firma, was ich sehr praktisch finde.

EXAM ALERT!

- Vocabulary learnt in Key Stage 3 can be helpful in activities like this, so make sure you look back over your old books before the exam.
- The second part of the recording has the negative **nicht** before **jung** and it can be very easy not to hear this crucial word and therefore to select the wrong answer.

> Students have struggled with exam questions similar to this – **be prepared!**

Don't be put off by nouns made up from two or more familiar shorter nouns: **Autofirma** – car firm, **Radweg** – cycle path, **Wohnblock** – block of flats.

Now try this   LISTENING 51 target C

Listen to the rest of the recording and complete the activity.

What does Florian say are the **two** disadvantages of the job?

Write the correct letters from the sentences above in the boxes. ☐ ☐

Jobs

Make sure you know both the male and female versions of the jobs listed below.

Jobs

Arzt/Ärztin
doctor

Bauer/Bäuerin
farmer

Briefträger/in
postman/woman

Elektriker/in
electrician

Feuerwehrmann /
Feuerwehrfrau
fireman/woman

Fleischer/in / Metzger/in
butcher

Ingenieur/in
engineer

Klempner/in
plumber

Krankenpfleger /
Krankenschwester
nurse

Mechaniker/in
mechanic

Polizist/in
police officer

Sekretär/in
secretary

Tischler/in
carpenter/
joiner

Verkäufer/in
salesperson

Masculine and feminine forms

Ich möchte Lehrer werden.
I would like to be a teacher. (male)

Ich möchte Lehrerin werden.
I would like to be a teacher. (female)

Ich bin Zahnarzt.
I am a dentist. (male)

Ich bin Zahnärztin.
I am a dentist. (female)

Hausfrau / Hausmann
housewife / husband

Kaufmann / Kauffrau
businessman / woman

No need for the word for 'a' with jobs in German.

Worked example

 LISTENING 52 target B

Listen to Lars talking about his family.
How many sisters does he have? 2

– Ich stelle dir meine Familie vor. Meine ältere Schwester arbeitet als Krankenschwester und spielt unheimlich gern Tennis. Meine andere Schwester heißt Carmen.

You have to wait some time to get the answer to this question. Don't jump to the conclusion that Lars only has one sister. Carry on listening and you will hear him mention **eine andere Schwester** (another sister).

Listening tips

- Read the questions BEFORE you listen.
- JOT DOWN words in English or German as you listen – you can then write the answer neatly in English after the recording has stopped.
- Watch out for any questions requiring TWO pieces of information.

Now try this

  LISTENING 53 target B

Questions 2 and 3 ask for **details** about his parents' jobs. Do not give any extra information you might hear about their hobbies, characteristics, etc. It is **not** relevant.

Listen to further details. Answer the questions in English.
1 (a) What job does Carmen have?
  (b) What hours does she work?
2 What does Lars say about his mother's job? Give **two** details.
3 What does Lars say about his father's job? Give **two** details.

Job adverts

Learn the prepositions below as well as the job advert vocabulary.

Stellenanzeigen

Angestellte (m/f)	employee
Arbeit (f)	work
Bedingungen (fpl)	conditions
Arbeitgeber (m)	employer
Betrieb (m)	company
Bewerbung (f)	application
Bezahlung (f)	pay
Euro pro Stunde	euros per hour
Gehalt (n)	salary
Kandidat/in (m/f)	candidate
Kündigung (f)	resignation
Lebenslauf (m)	CV
Stelle (f)	job
sich um eine Stelle bewerben	to apply for a job
bereit	ready / prepared
freundlich	friendly

Genitive prepositions

Grammar page 86

The following all take the genitive case:

außerhalb	outside, beyond
statt	instead of
trotz	despite
während	during
wegen	due to, because of

(m) der Arbeitsgeber – statt **des** Arbeitsgeber**s**

(f) die Pause – während **der** Pause

(n) das Gehalt – trotz **des** Gehalt**s**

Genitive = possession: you cannot add an apostrophe 's': my dad's job = der Job meines Vaters

Ich bin der Chef der Firma.

Worked example

target C

Read the job adverts.

A Für unser Team suchen wir erfahrene Verkäufer/innen. Gutes Gehalt und erstklassige Arbeitsbedingungen vorhanden.

B Wir suchen qualifizierte Klempner, die uns bei den Kücheninstallationen helfen können.

C Kindergarten sucht Putzhilfe. Montag bis Freitag, abends. Gute Arbeitsbedingungen.

D Freundliche und geschäftige Tierarztpraxis sucht Hilfe.

E Sie sind verantwortlich für die Online-Aktivitäten des Unternehmens. Schicken Sie uns Ihren Lebenslauf.

F Bewerben Sie sich bei uns, wenn Sie eine Karriere in der Motorindustrie suchen …

Which advert matches this jobseeker?

Josef would like a job as a plumber. ☐ B

Reading tips

- Underline the jobs in the adverts and see how many of them you know.
- If you don't recognise the jobs vocabulary, look at what other clues are given in each advert, such as cognates and parts of the word being familiar, e.g. Putzhilfe, which is connected to the verb putzen (to clean), so it means 'help with the cleaning', i.e. cleaner.

Now try this

Which advert from above matches these jobseekers?

1 Sonia is a computer expert. ☐   **2** Peter is a sales assistant. ☐   **3** Karola is a trained vet. ☐

CV

You may want to include some details of a CV in your writing assessment.

Der Lebenslauf

Persönliche Daten (Personal details): ....

Geburtsdatum und –ort (Date of birth/place): ....

Schulausbildung (Education): ....

Berufsausbildung (Training): ....

Arbeitserfahrung (Work experience): ....

Sonstiges (Other): ....

Zurzeit besuche ich die ... Schule.
I am currently attending the ... school.

Ich interessiere mich für Segeln und Musik.
I am interested in sailing and music.

Ich hoffe, eines Tages, Rechtsanwalt /
Rechtsanwältin zu werden.
One day I hope to become a lawyer.

Etwas, nichts, wenig + adjective

Try to include some of these higher level phrases where the adjective has a capital letter:

viel Interessantes	a lot of interesting things
etwas Spannendes	something exciting

wenig Gutes	not much / little good
nichts Besonderes	nothing special

Worked example

Write a personal statement for your CV.

Mein Geburtsdatum ist der elfte August 1999. Ich habe immer in Bath in Südwestengland gewohnt und zurzeit besuche ich die St.-Thomas-Schule.

 AIMING HIGHER

Ich bin am 11. August 1999 in Bath geboren. Ich ging fünf Jahre lang in die St.-Thomas-Schule und ich habe in zehn Fächern gute Noten bekommen.
Für das Arbeitspraktikum habe ich eine Stelle in einem Gartenbetrieb gefunden. Ich interessiere mich wahnsinnig für Pflanzen und arbeite am liebsten im Freien. Ich würde sagen, dass ich freundlich, geduldig, sportlich und ziemlich selbstbewusst bin. Ich bin auch ehrgeizig und möchte eines Tages eine erfolgreiche Karriere machen.

Writing strategies

- You can use CV headings to write a biography of a famous person. Instead of ich bin / habe, use er / sie hat / ist.
- DON'T overcomplicate your work – stick to structures you are familiar with.
- BUT don't overuse the same verbs: ist / war, hat / hatte and es gibt / gab are great, but don't use them all the time.
- DON'T write long lists, for example of different subjects.
- Be VERY careful if you are using a dictionary in the exam – only use it as a last resort for a key word, otherwise stick to the vocabulary you are familiar with.

Now try this

Copy the six headings from the CV at the top of the page and prepare a few sentences about each one in German.

Ich bin am ... in ... geboren.
Meine Lieblingsfächer sind ...., weil ...
Ich habe Erfahrung als ... Ich habe ...
In den Sommerferien habe / bin ich ...
Nächstes Jahr werde ich ...

Job application

Make sure you are familiar with letter-writing conventions, as you may meet them when reading a job application.

Die Bewerbung

Ich lege meinen Lebenslauf bei.   I enclose my CV.

Ich möchte vom 21. Juli bis zum 1. September arbeiten.
I would like to work from 21 July to 1 September.

Ich habe ausgezeichnete Sprachkenntnisse.
I have excellent language skills.

Letzten Sommer habe ich als Verkäuferin gearbeitet.
Last summer I worked as a sales assistant.

Ich hoffe, später im Ausland zu arbeiten.
Later, I hope to work abroad.

Letztes Jahr habe ich als Eisverkäuferin gearbeitet.
Last year I worked as an ice-cream seller.

Letter writing conventions

Sehr geehrter Herr X
Dear + man's name

Sehr geehrte Frau Y
Dear + woman's name

Vielen Dank im Voraus
With thanks in advance

Mit bestem Gruß
With best wishes

Mit freundlichen Grüßen
Yours sincerely

Alles Gute
All the best

Worked example

Read Nancy's job application letter.

Ich möchte ab dem 13. Dezember sechs Wochen lang arbeiten. Ich bin sehr sportlich und kann gut Ski sowie Snowboard fahren. Ich spreche Englisch, Deutsch und Italienisch.

Letzten Sommer habe ich in einem Kinderferienklub im Schwarzwald gearbeitet. Es war klasse, obwohl die Arbeitsstunden lang waren und das Wetter schlecht war.

Ich hoffe, später ein Jahr bei Verwandten in Manchester zu verbringen, um mein Englisch zu verbessern.

Read the statement. Write **T** (true), **F** (false) or **?** (Not in the text).

Nancy is applying for a summer job.   ☐ F

Reading tips

- PACE YOURSELF so you don't run out of time – this is a short letter, so don't spend hours pondering what a word means, especially if that word is not needed to answer the questions.

- BE PREPARED for vocabulary from a variety of topic areas to come up in any reading passage. This one is a job application, but many of the words have little to do with jobs.

- Work out the meaning of **Ferienklub** (holiday club) by breaking it up.

- If you don't know what **Verwandte** (relatives) means, you might know that it is not a penfriend (**Brieffreundin**).

Now try this

Read the text again and write **T** (True), **F** (False) or **?** (Not in the text) for these statements.

(a) Nancy finds skiing tiring.   ☐
(b) Nancy can speak three languages.   ☐
(c) Nancy has never had a holiday job before.   ☐
(d) Her experience of work has been positive and negative.   ☐
(e) Nancy hopes to stay with a penfriend in England.   ☐

Job interview

Here you can prepare for a speaking task by role-playing a job interview.

 Sie du

Das Bewerbungsgespräch

Ich möchte ein Jahr in Deutschland verbringen, um mein Deutsch zu verbessern.
I would like to spend a year in Germany to improve my German.

Ich komme gut mit anderen Menschen aus.
I get on well with other people.

Im Sommer habe ich die Schule mit dem Abschlusszeugnis verlassen.
I left school in the summer with the leaving certificate.

Letztes Jahr habe ich zwei Wochen bei einer internationalen Firma verbracht.
Last year I spent two weeks with an international firm.

Ich habe viel gelernt.
I learnt a lot.

Ich möchte bei Ihnen Erfahrungen sammeln.
I would like to gain experience with you.

Different words for 'you'

Familiar

du = 'you' to another young person, family member / friend, animal

ihr = 'you' plural of du

Formal

Sie = 'you' to adult(s), teacher(s), official(s)

Sie = singular and plural

Examiner = Sie!!!

Questions in a job interview

Wie sind die Arbeitsstunden?
What are the hours?

Gibt es gute Aufstiegsmöglichkeiten?
Are there good promotion prospects?

Muss ich am Wochenende arbeiten?
Do I have to work at the weekend?

Worked example SPEAKING LISTENING 54

Task: a job interview

You have applied to spend six months working in an Austrian ski resort.

Your teacher is going to ask you about:

- why you want to work abroad;
- your characteristics;
- your education;
- work experience;
- ! (A question for which you have not prepared.)

Listen to the interview. You can read the script on the Pearson website at www.pearsonschools.co.uk/mflrevisionaudio

CONTROLLED ASSESSMENT

You might be surprised to learn that native speakers do not always score the highest grades for their speaking assessments – their pronunciation may be flawless, but top grades also need a variety of structures, tenses and vocabulary to be used throughout the task.

- The student gives more than one answer to the question. Avoid really short answers – the longer you speak, the more control you have over the interview.
- The student speaks clearly and slowly. Don't rush!

Now try this SPEAKING

Imagine you are applying for a summer job as a tour guide in Munich. Prepare answers in German to these questions you might be asked.

- Warum willst du den Sommer im Ausland verbringen?
- Warum meinst du, dass du für diese Stelle geeignet bist?
- Hast du schon einmal ein Arbeitspraktikum gemacht?
- Was hoffst du, in Zukunft zu tun?

Opinions about jobs

The opinions on this page can equally well be applied to other topic areas – holidays, school, visits ...

Meinungen über die Arbeit

Angestellte (m/f)	employee
Arbeitszeit (f)	work time
Begeisterung (f)	enthusiasm
Beruf (m)	job
Besitzer (m)	owner
Ganztagsjob (m)	full-time job
empfehlen	to recommend
kündigen	to hand in your notice
arbeitslos	unemployed
berufstätig	employed
ganztags	full-time
gut / schlecht bezahlt	well / badly paid
Es macht viel Spaß.	It is great fun.
Es gefällt mir (sehr).	I enjoy it (a lot).
Ich fühle mich wohl.	I feel comfortable.
Ein Vorteil ist, dass ...	An advantage is that ...

Giving opinions

Meiner Meinung nach + verb next ...

In my opinion ...

Meiner Meinung nach sind die Bedingungen prima.

In my opinion the conditions are excellent.

Other words for 'to think':

finden   denken   meinen   glauben

Ich finde, dass manche Arbeitgeber gemein sind.

I think that many employers are mean.

Ich denke, dass viele Nebenjobs schlecht bezahlt sind.

I think that a lot of part-time jobs are badly paid.

Positive und negative Meinungen

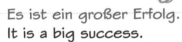

👍

Es ist ein großer Erfolg.
It is a big success.

Ich wäre gern noch länger geblieben.
I would have liked to stay longer.

Ihre Begeisterung und Ehrlichkeit haben mir sehr imponiert.
Their enthusiasm and honesty impressed me a lot.

👎

kaputt / erschöpft	broken / exhausted
ermüdend	tiring
endlos	endless
Es ärgert mich sehr.	It really annoys me.
Es ist entsetzlich.	It is terrible.
Ich würde es niemandem empfehlen.	I wouldn't recommend it to anyone.

Worked example

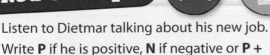 LISTENING 55 target B

Listen to Dietmar talking about his new job. Write **P** if he is positive, **N** if negative or **P + N** if he is both.

☐ P

– Mein neuer Job gefällt mir sehr und macht mir besonders Spaß, weil meine Kollegen alle jung und dynamisch sind.

Understanding opinions

Many listening activities rely on you understanding the OPINION given. Listen for CLUES such as the speaker's intonation to help you identify whether they are being positive or negative.

Now try this

  LISTENING 60 target B

Listen to **five** more opinions and decide if they are positive, negative or both.

Don't be misled by the word **Probleme** in number 4. It is linked with **keine** (no), so maybe it is a positive opinion after all.

Part-time work

Vocabulary for part-time work may come up in passages about the world of work, so it is worth learning some of these phrases.

Der Nebenjob

Ich arbeite samstags als …
I work Saturdays as a …

Bauarbeiter (m)

Friseur / Friseuse (m/f)

Gärtner/in (m/f)

Kassierer/in (m/f)   Kellner/in (m/f)   Tellerwäscher (m/f)

Verkäufer/in (m/f)   Ich babysitte.   Ich trage Zeitungen aus.

This, each, every, which

> Grammar page 88

These follow the pattern of der, die, das.

dieser	this	jener	that
jeder	every	welcher?	which?

	nom	acc	dat
masc	dieser	diesen	diesem
fem	diese	diese	dieser
neut	dieses	dieses	diesem
plural	diese	diese	diesen

(m acc) Welchen Job würdest du lieber machen?
Which job would you prefer to do?

(f acc) Ich finde jede Arbeit anstrengend.
I find every job tiring.

(n dat) Ich möchte in diesem Restaurant arbeiten.
I would like to work in this restaurant.

Worked example

READING · target A*

Read this article about part-time jobs.

> Vielen Jugendlichen reicht das Taschengeld heutzutage nicht aus, weil ihr Wunsch nach trendigen Kleidungsstücken oder technischen Geräten immer größer wird. Die Lösung? Einen Nebenjob suchen. Obwohl die Möglichkeiten zahlreich sind – von Regale im lokalen Supermarkt auffüllen bis zur Aushilfe im nahe gelegenen Café – muss man oft älter sein, um manche Stellen zu bekommen. Man muss zum Beispiel 18 sein, um im Kino oder in einer Kneipe arbeiten zu dürfen. Die Suche wird sich aber lohnen, denn die erste Arbeitssuche ist ein wichtiger Schritt in Richtung Selbstständigkeit.

Why is pocket money not enough for many teenagers?

They want the latest clothes / gadgets.

Aiming higher – reading

- READ texts like this for detail – it is no good just picking out a key word and repeating it for your answer at this level.

- SPOTTING a key word or cognate in a higher level text might well lead you to the answer – but it is rarely the answer itself. You need to understand the language surrounding that key word and thus find the answer.

Now try this

READING · target A*

Answer these questions on the above text.

(a) What solution is suggested to the problem?
(b) Which **two** jobs are suggested for teenagers?
(c) Why can't some teenagers get a job in a bar?
(d) Why is getting a part-time job viewed as being important?

Work experience

Writing about your work experience provides a good opportunity to use the past tense.

Das Arbeitspraktikum

Ich habe im Büro / Reisebüro gearbeitet.
I worked in an office / travel agency.

Ich habe jeden Tag im Geschäft gearbeitet.
I worked every day in a shop.

Ich fand, das war eine positive / negative Erfahrung.
I found it a positive / negative experience.

Es war eine einmalige Gelegenheit, in einer Werkstatt zu arbeiten.
It was a unique opportunity to work in a workshop.

Ich habe eine Woche in einer Fabrik verbracht.
I spent a week in a factory.

Ich habe Anrufe beantwortet.
I answered calls.

Ich habe Briefe geschrieben.
I wrote letters.

Saying 'somebody' and 'nobody'

JEMAND – somebody
Jemand hat mir geholfen.
Somebody helped me.

NIEMAND – nobody
Niemand möchte hier arbeiten.
Nobody wants to work here.

accusative = für jemanden / niemanden
dative = mit jemandem / niemandem

 Worked example WRITING target **B-A**

Was hast du beim Arbeitspraktikum gemacht?

Mein Arbeitspraktikum habe ich zwei Wochen lang in einem Büro verbracht, wo mein Onkel als Informatiker arbeitet. Ich fand die Erfahrung toll, obwohl der Tag viel länger als der typische Schultag war.

AIMING HIGHER
Am ersten Tag musste ich an der Rezeption arbeiten. Das war sehr kompliziert, aber glücklicherweise waren die Kollegen alle sehr freundlich und geduldig. Niemand war böse, als ich ein paar Fehler gemacht habe. Ich denke, dass ich in Zukunft gern in einem Büro arbeiten würde. Mein Ziel ist es, eines Tages meine eigene Firma zu haben, damit ich keinen Chef habe.

- This is a good piece of writing. It starts with a simple inversion and **Time before Place** sentence.
- It then continues with an **opinion** and the structure **obwohl** + comparison of school and working day.

- To aim for a top grade, you have to go the extra mile and give plenty of details and facts, using a good range of **vocabulary**, **structures** and **tenses**.

beibringen – to teach
böse – angry
mein Ziel ist es, … – it's my aim …

 Now try this WRITING

Look at the mind map and prepare an answer for each point in German.

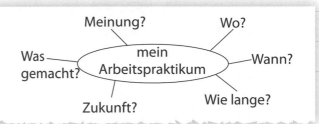

Meinung?   Wo?
Was gemacht? — mein Arbeitspraktikum — Wann?
Zukunft?   Wie lange?

My work experience

Use the phrases on this page to help you talk about your work experience.

Das Arbeitspraktikum

Ich habe ...

Kunden angerufen.

Kaffee gekocht.

kopiert.

Ich musste ...	I had to ...
Termine organisieren.	organise appointments.
Nachrichten ausrichten.	pass on messages.
Kunden zurückrufen.	phone clients back.

Ich hatte viel / wenig / keinen Kontakt zu Kunden.

I had lots of / little / no contact with clients.

Die Erfahrung war höchst interessant.
The experience was really interesting.

Ich war sehr / nicht beschäftigt.
I was very / not busy.

Adverbs of time

Usually, the verb must come second:

Dann habe ich den Kaffee gekocht.
Then I made coffee.

danach	afterwards	vorher	beforehand
dann	then	zuerst	first of all

With bevor and nachdem the verb goes to the end:

Bevor ich mit der Aufgabe angefangen habe, musste ich mit dem Chef sprechen.

Before I started the task, I had to speak with the boss.

Nachdem ich versehentlich die E-Mails gelöscht hatte, waren die Mitarbeiter nicht mehr so freundlich.

After I had unintentionally deleted the emails, my colleagues weren't so friendly any more.

Worked example

Which of these sentences best expresses Liane's attitude to her work experience?

A It was relevant to her future career.
B It didn't give an insight into the workplace.
C It was not challenging enough.

Write the correct letter in the box. ☐ C

– Ja, richtig. Eine interessante Erfahrung war das, muss ich wohl sagen, und zumindest weiß ich jetzt, dass ich ganz sicherlich nicht im Kaufhaus arbeiten möchte. Ich habe alles über eine Karriere im Kaufsektor gelernt, und obwohl das Praktikum interessant war, fand ich die Arbeit ein bisschen zu einfach.

Multiple choice questions

- This sort of multiple choice task challenges students aiming for the higher grades.

- It's easy to be put off as items in all three options are mentioned.

- To get the correct answer, you have to understand detail in the use of adverbs, qualifiers, negatives and tenses.

If you understand alles über eine Karriere im Kaufsektor gelernt, you will be well on the way to getting the correct answer and discounting option B. Using further deduction, you can work out it can't be A (because she doesn't want to work in a shop).

Now try this

Listen and note the correct answer for Devis. ☐

A He enjoyed the office atmosphere. B His colleagues were too busy to help him.
C He had a lot of time on his hands.

Gender and plurals

When you are learning a German noun, always learn it with its word for 'the' (gender).
All German words are masculine, feminine or neuter.

Der, die, das (the)

Every German noun is masculine
(m – der), feminine (f – die) or neuter
(n – das).

Der Mann ist groß.
The man is tall.

Die Frau ist klug.
The woman is clever.

Das Kind ist nervig.
The child is annoying.

Die Katzen sind süß.
The cats are cute.

	masc	fem	neut	pl
Nominative	der	die	das	die

If you don't know the gender of a word,
you can look it up in a dictionary.

Mann [man] *m* man

Der, die, das as the subject

The definite articles der, die, das, die are
used when the noun is the SUBJECT of the
sentence. That means it is doing the action
of the verb.

Der Lehrer spielt Fußball.
The teacher is playing football.

This is called the NOMINATIVE case.

Look at page 86 for more details
of the cases in German.

Der, die, das as the object

BUT if the teacher becomes the OBJECT of
the verb, i.e. is seen by someone else, then
DER changes to DEN.

Ich sehe den Lehrer.   I see the teacher.

I = subject, as it is doing the seeing, and the
teacher is the object, as he is being seen.

This is called the ACCUSATIVE case – die and
das stay the same when used in this way.

	masc	fem	neut	pl
Accusative	den	die	das	die

Plurals

German nouns have different plurals. Not
sure what they are? Check in a dictionary.

Mann [man] (¨er) *m* man

The part in brackets tells you what to add to make the word plural.
The umlaut before the -er ending tells you that an umlaut is added to
the vowel before the ending, so the plural of **Mann** is **Männer**.

Now try this

Which definite article – **der**, **die** or **das**? Use a
dictionary to find the gender and plural of these nouns.

(a) Anmeldung
(b) Fahrer
(c) Rührei
(d) Haltestelle
(e) Fernseher
(f) Brötchen

The gender is taken from the last
word of compound nouns: der Abend
+ das Brot = das Abendbrot.

Cases 1

Prepositions such as durch (through) and zu (to) trigger a change in der, die or das, as they have to be followed by a specific case – the accusative, dative or genitive.

Changes to 'the'

	masc	fem	neut	pl
Nominative	der	die	das	die
Accusative	den	die	das	die
Dative	dem	der	dem	den
Genitive	des	der	des	der

Changes to 'a'

	masc	fem	neut	pl
Nominative	ein	eine	ein	keine
Accusative	einen	eine	ein	keine
Dative	einem	einer	einem	keinen
Genitive	eines	einer	eines	keiner

The genitive is not used that often, but it looks impressive if you can use it correctly!

keine – not a / no

Prepositions + accusative

Prepositions which trigger a change to the ACCUSATIVE case:

für	for
um	around
durch	through
gegen	against / towards
entlang	along
bis	until
ohne	without

FUDGEBO = first letters of all accusative prepositions!

Ich kaufe ein Geschenk für einen Freund.

I am buying a present for a friend.

Geh um die Ecke.
Go round the corner.

Prepositions + dative

Prepositions which trigger a change to the DATIVE case:

aus	from	nach	after
außer	except	seit	since
bei	at, at the home of	von	from
gegenüber	opposite	zu	to
mit	with		

nach einer Weile
after a while

Fahr mit dem Bus.
Go by bus.

zu + dem = zum
zu + der = zur
bei + dem = beim

• You need to add -n to the end of a plural masculine or neuter noun in the dative case:

mit meinen Freunden = with my friends.

Prepositions + genitive

Prepositions which trigger a change to the GENITIVE case:

laut	according to
trotz	in spite of
wegen	because of
während	during
wegen des Wetters	because of the weather

You also need to add an -s to the end of a masculine or neuter noun in the genitive case.

Now try this

Translate these phrases into German by adding the preposition and changing the word for 'the' or 'a'.

(a) against the wall (die Mauer)
(b) except one child (ein Kind)
(c) despite the snow (der Schnee)
(d) after an hour (eine Stunde)

(e) to the shops (die Geschäfte – pl)
(f) without a word (ein Wort)
(g) during the summer (der Sommer)
(h) at the doctor's (der Arzt)

Cases 2

Movement TOWARDS or not? That is the key question with this group of prepositions, which can be followed by either the accusative or the dative case.

Dual case prepositions

an	at
auf	on
hinter	behind
in	in
neben	next to
über	over
unter	under
vor	in front of
zwischen	between

- If there is movement towards a place, these prepositions trigger a change to the ACCUSATIVE case.

  Ich gehe ins Haus. = I go into the house.

- If there is NO movement towards a place, these prepositions trigger a change to the DATIVE case.

  Ich bin im Haus. =
  I am in the house.

  in + das = ins
  in + dem = im

Verbs + accusative

Some verbs work with a preposition which is followed by the accusative case.

aufpassen auf	to look after
sich gewöhnen an	to get used to
sich streiten über	to argue about
sich erinnern an	to remember
sich freuen auf	to look forward to

warten auf   to wait for

Ich muss auf den Hund aufpassen.
I have to look after the dog.

Ich freue mich auf den Sommer.
I am looking forward to the summer.

Ich habe mich an die Arbeit gewöhnt.
I have got used to the work.

Prepositional phrases

Die Katze springt auf den Tisch. (acc)   The cat jumps onto the table.
Die Katze sitzt auf dem Tisch. (dat)   The cat is sitting on the table.
Ich surfe gern im Internet. (dat)   I like surfing the net.
Sie wohnt auf dem Land. (dat)   She lives in the countryside.
auf der linken Seite (dat)   on the left-hand side

As you can see here, where there is **no movement** the dual case preposition is generally followed by the **dative** case, and where there is a sense of **movement** it is followed by the **accusative**.

Now try this

Complete the sentences with the correct definite article ('the').

(a) Ich wohne an .... Küste (f).

(b) Sie streiten sich über .... Fernseher (m).

(c) Was gibt es hinter .... Haus (n)?

(d) Wie finden Sie die Geschichte über .... Jungen (pl)?

(e) Die Nacht vor .... Hochzeit (f).

(f) Man muss zwischen .... Zeilen (pl) lesen.

(g) Denke an .... Namen (m sing).

(h) Erinnerst du dich an .... Person (f)?

Cases 3

Other groups of words, such as adjectives, also change according to case.

Words that follow the der, die, das pattern

These words follow the pattern of der, die, das:

dieser (this)   jeder (each)   jener (that)
mancher (some) solcher (such) welcher (which)

dieser Mann   this man
bei jeder Gelegenheit at every opportunity
jedes Mal   every time

	masc	fem	neut	pl
Nominative	dieser	diese	dieses	diese
Accusative	diesen	diese	dieses	diese
Dative	diesem	dieser	diesem	diesen

Ways to use these words

dieses und jenes	this and that
in dieser Hinsicht	in this respect
jeder Einzelne	every individual
jeder Zweite	every other
zu jener Zeit / Stunde	at that time / hour
mancher Besucher	many a visitor
Mit solchen Leuten will ich nichts zu tun haben.	I don't want to have anything to do with such people.
Welche Größe haben Sie?	What size are you?

Words that follow the ein pattern

These words follow the pattern of ein:

kein (not a)
mein (my)   unser (our)
dein (your)   euer (your, plural)
sein (his)   Ihr (your, polite)
ihr (her)   ihr (their)

	masc	fem	neut	pl
Nominative	kein	keine	kein	keine
Accusative	keinen	keine	kein	keine
Dative	keinem	keiner	keinem	keinen

ich habe keine Lust – I don't want to + infinitive with zu

meiner Meinung nach (dat) – in my opinion

Ways to use these words

keine Ahnung	no idea
mein Fehler	my mistake
gib dein Bestes	do your best
sein ganzes Leben	his whole life
ihr Ziel ist es …	it's her / their aim …
als unser Vertreter	as our representative
auf euren Handys	on your mobiles
Ihr Zeichen	your reference
für ihre Schularbeit	for their schoolwork

Now try this

Translate the sentences into English.

(a) Ich habe keine Lust, einkaufen zu gehen.
(b) Sie hat ihr ganzes Taschengeld für Kleidung ausgegeben.
(c) Viele Leute werden schnell unhöflich.
(d) Ich finde mein Leben langweilig.
(e) Dieses Mal fahren wir mit dem Zug.
(f) Seine Eltern sind arbeitslos.
(g) Solche Regeln finde ich dumm.
(h) Welches Buch liest du?

Adjective endings

Refer to these tables when you are preparing for your spoken and written assessments to check your adjective endings are CORRECT!

Adjective endings with the definite article 'the'

You can also use these endings after dieser (this), jener (that), jeder (each), mancher (many), solcher (such) and welcher (which). The endings are either -e or -en!

	masc	fem	neut	pl
Nominative	der kleine Hund	die kleine Maus	das kleine Haus	die kleinen Kinder
Accusative	den kleinen Hund	die kleine Maus	das kleine Haus	die kleinen Kinder
Dative	dem kleinen Hund	der kleinen Maus	dem kleinen Haus	den kleinen Kindern

Siehst du den kleinen Hund? Can you see the little dog?

Adjective endings with the indefinite article 'a'

You can also use these endings after kein (not a), mein (my), dein (your), sein (his), ihr (her / their), unser (our) and euer (your pl).

	masc	fem	neut	pl
Nominative	ein kleiner Hund	eine kleine Maus	ein kleines Haus	meine kleinen Kinder
Accusative	einen kleinen Hund	eine kleine Maus	ein kleines Haus	meine kleinen Kinder
Dative	einem kleinen Hund	einer kleinen Maus	einem kleinen Haus	meinen kleinen Kindern

Ich wohne in einem kleinen Haus. I live in a little house.

Adjective endings with no article

	masc	fem	neut	pl
Nominative	kleiner Hund	kleine Maus	kleines Haus	kleine Kinder
Accusative	kleinen Hund	kleine Maus	kleines Haus	kleine Kinder
Dative	kleinem Hund	kleiner Maus	kleinem Haus	kleinen Kindern

Kleine Kinder sind oft süß. Little children are often cute.

Many of these are similar to the definite articles:
das Haus = kleines Haus,
der Mann = großer Mann.

Now try this

Complete the sentences using the adjectives in brackets with their correct endings.

(a) Ich habe .... Noten in Deutsch. (ausgezeichnet)

(b) Im Jugendklub kann ich .... Essen kaufen. (warm)

(c) Ich suche ein .... Bett. (preisgünstig)

(d) Die .... Lage war sehr praktisch. (zentral)

(e) Der Garten ist eine .... Raucherecke. (beliebt)

(f) Das ist eines der .... Lieder des Jahres. (meistverkauft)

(g) Letztes Wochenende gab es einen .... Sonntag. (verkaufsoffen)

(h) Stell keine .... Daten ins Netz. (persönlich)

Comparisons

To aim high, you will need to include comparatives and superlatives in your work, so always think of a way of making your assessments good, better ... best!

Formation

Add -er for the comparison, as in English (loud ➡ louder).

Add -(e)ste for the superlative 'most'.

Ich bin laut.   I am loud.

Ich bin lauter als du.
I am louder than you.

Ich bin die lauteste Person.
I am the loudest person.

- Adjectives are the same as adverbs, so you can compare how somebody does something very easily.

Ich schreie laut.	I shout loudly.
Ich schreie lauter als du.	I shout more loudly than you.
Ich schreie am lautesten.	I shout the loudest.

- Comparative and superlative adjectives have to agree with the noun they are describing.

| die schöneren Ohrringe | the prettier earrings |
| der lustigste Junge | the funniest boy |

Irregular comparatives

Some adjectives have small changes in the comparative and superlative forms.

alt old	➡ älter older	➡ älteste oldest
jung young	➡ jünger younger	➡ jüngste youngest
groß big	➡ größer bigger	➡ größte biggest
gut good	➡ besser better	➡ beste best
lang long	➡ länger longer	➡ längste longest
hoch high	➡ höher higher	➡ höchste highest

Gern, lieber, am liebsten

Use gern (like), lieber (prefer) and am liebsten (like most of all) to compare your likes and dislikes.

gern and lieber go after the verb:

Ich spiele gern Schach.
I like playing chess.

Ich schwimme lieber.
I prefer swimming.

Use am liebsten to start your sentence:

Am liebsten fahre ich Ski. ♥♥♥
Most of all I like skiing.

Lieblingssport – favourite sport
Lieblingsgruppe – favourite group

Now try this

Complete the sentences with a comparative or superlative form.

(a) Mathe ist viel .... als Chemie. (einfach)
(b) Mein Bruder ist .... als meine Schwester. (jung)
(c) Dieses Lied ist doch .... als der letzte Schlager. (gut)
(d) Meiner Meinung nach ist Physik .... als Chemie. (nützlich)
(e) Ich habe das .... Zimmer im Haus. (klein)
(f) Das .... Fach in der Schule ist Informatik. (langweilig)
(g) Meine Stadt ist das .... Urlaubsziel in Deutschland. (beliebt)
(h) Letztes Jahr hatte ich die .... Noten der Klasse. (schlecht)

Personal pronouns

Just like der, die, das, pronouns change depending on which case they are in – the nominative, accusative or dative case.

Pronouns

Pronouns = he, him, their, her, she, etc.

Nominative	Accusative	Dative
ich	mich	mir
du	dich	dir
er / sie / es	ihn / sie / es	ihm / ihr / ihm
wir	uns	uns
ihr	euch	euch
Sie / sie	Sie / sie	Ihnen / ihnen

- Use PRONOUNS to avoid repeating nouns.

  Ich mag Dieter, weil er nett ist.
  I like Dieter because he is nice.

- When a noun is the ACCUSATIVE OBJECT of the sentence, you need to use the ACCUSATIVE PRONOUN: Ich sehe ihn.
  I see him.

- Use the correct pronoun after prepositions, depending on whether they take the accusative or dative case.

  bei mir (dat)   at my house

  für ihn (acc)   for him

Dative pronoun phrases

These expressions need a dative pronoun.

Es tut mir leid.	I am sorry.	Wie geht's dir / Ihnen?	How are you?
Es gefällt ihm.	He likes it.	Es geht uns gut.	We are well.
Es fällt mir schwer.	I find it difficult.	Es hilft ihnen.	It helps them.
Es tut ihr weh.	It hurts her.	Es scheint ihnen, dass ...	It seems to them that ...
Das schmeckt mir.	That tastes good.		
Sport macht ihr Spaß.	She finds sport fun.	Das ist uns egal.	We don't mind about that.

Sie or du?

Familiar

du = 'you' to another young person, family member / friend, animal

ihr = 'you' plural of du (more than one young person)

Formal

Sie = 'you' to adult(s), teacher(s), official(s)

sie = singular and plural

Sie / du

Now try this

Choose the correct pronoun.

(a) Nina ist sympathisch, obwohl .... manchmal auch launisch ist.

(b) Es tut .... leid, aber ich kann nicht zur Party kommen.

(c) Seit wann geht es .... schlecht, Leon?

(d) Wir sind ins Theater gegangen, aber leider hat .... das Stück nicht gefallen.

(e) Mein Freund geht .... auf die Nerven, aber ich will nicht mit .... Schluss machen.

(f) Hast du Zeit, ... bei den Hausaufgaben zu helfen?

Had a look ☐ Nearly there ☐ Nailed it! ☐

Word order

German word order follows rules – learn the rules and your sentences will be in the correct order!

Verb in second place

VERB never comes first – it is always in second place!

❶ Ich **❷** fahre **❸** mit dem Auto.

❶ Jeden Tag **❷** fahre ich **❸** mit dem Auto.

Perfect tense

Form of haben / sein goes in second position:

❶ Gestern **❷** bin ich **❸** mit dem Auto **❹** gefahren.

Future tense

Form of werden goes in second position:

❶ Morgen **❷** werde ich **❸** mit dem Auto **❹** fahren.

Modals

Form of modal goes in second position:

❶ Ich **❷** will **❸** mit dem Auto **❹** fahren.

> Remember!
> ich werde – I will / I am going to
> ich will – I want to

Time – Manner – Place

A detail of transport counts as Manner, so put it after a Time expression, but before a Place.

T gestern / heute / letzte Woche / in Zukunft

M mit dem Zug / zu Fuß / mit meiner Familie

P nach London / in die Stadt / über die Brücke

T Ich fahre heute
Today I am going

M mit dem Zug
by train

P nach Bonn.
to Bonn.

Linking words

No word order change here!

| aber | but | oder | or |
| denn | because | und | and |

Ich spiele gern Tennis und ich fahre gern Rad.
I like playing tennis and I like cycling.

Ich esse gern Pommes, aber ich esse nicht gern Bratkartoffeln.
I like eating chips but I don't like roast potatoes.

Now try this

Order the sentences following the above rules.

(a) fahre / ich / ins Ausland / gern
(b) Verkehrsamt / findet / Informationen / beim / man
(c) gesund / ich / normalerweise / esse
(d) sehen / manchmal / Filme / wir / im Jugendklub
(e) arbeiten / ich / im Sportzentrum / möchte / im Juli
(f) habe gearbeitet / ich / in einem Büro / letztes Jahr
(g) gehe / ins Kino / mit meiner Mutter / morgen / ich

> Try to invert your sentences by starting with a time expression rather than **ich, du,** etc.

Conjunctions

You will be expected to use plenty of conjunctions like weil, wenn and als in your spoken assessment – and you will HAVE to show you can use them correctly!

Verb to the end

Weil (because) sends the verb ➡ to the END.

Ich rede über Beyonce, weil sie meine Lieblingssängerin ist.
I am talking about Beyonce because she is my favourite singer.

Ich gehe nicht gern ins Kino, weil das zu teuer ist.
I don't like going to the cinema because it is too expensive.

All these conjunctions also send the verb to the end of the clause, just like weil.

als	when (one occasion, past tense)	nachdem	after
		ob	whether
bevor	before	obwohl	although
bis	until	während	while
da	because / since	was	what
		wie	how
damit	so that	wenn	when / if (present or future)
dass	that		
		wo	where

Perfect tense

• In the PERFECT tense, the form of haben / sein is LAST in a clause.

Ich kann nicht zur Party kommen, obwohl ich meine Hausaufgaben gemacht habe.
I can't come to the party although I have done my homework.

• Watch out for the VERB, COMMA, VERB structure.

Als ich klein war, habe ich viel im Garten gespielt.
When I was small, I played in the garden a lot.

Future tense and modals

• In the FUTURE tense, it is the form of werden which goes last.

Da ich nach Afrika reisen werde, muss ich zum Arzt.
Because I am going to travel to Africa, I have to go to the doctor.

• With MODAL verbs, it is the modal itself which is last in the clause.

Ich bin immer glücklich, wenn ich ins Konzert gehen darf.
I am always happy when I am allowed to go to the concert.

Now try this

Form of modal ➡ right to the end; form of haben / sein in the perfect tense ➡ right to the end!

Join these sentences with the subordinating conjunction in brackets.

(a) Ich habe bei meiner Großmutter gewohnt. Meine Mutter war im Krankenhaus. (während)

(b) Ich bin ins Café gegangen. Ich habe ein T-Shirt gekauft. (nachdem)

(c) Ich war in Spanien im Urlaub. Ich habe einen neuen Freund kennen gelernt. (als)

(d) Er ist sehr beliebt. Er ist nicht sehr freundlich. (obwohl)

(e) Ich werde auf eine neue Gitarre sparen. Ich finde einen Nebenjob. (wenn)

(f) Ich bin froh. Ich habe in der Schule gute Noten bekommen. (dass)

(g) Ich muss meine Eltern fragen. Ich darf ins Konzert gehen. (ob)

More on word order

There are a few more structures here which you should try and fit into your work to improve your writing and speaking. They also affect word order, so be careful!

Using um ... zu ...

Um ... zu ... means 'in order to' and is used in German where we might just say 'to'. It requires an infinitive verb at the end of the clause.

Ich trage Zeitungen aus, um Geld zu verdienen.

> infinitive verb

I deliver newspapers, (in order) to earn money.

- Only use um ... zu ... where you would say 'in order to' in English, even if you drop the 'in order' bit.
- The verb after um ... zu ... is always in the infinitive and at the END.
- Add a comma before um.

ohne ... zu ... = without, and works in the same way.
Ich bin in die Schule gegangen, ohne ihn zu sehen. I went to school without seeing him.

Infinitive expressions

These expressions with zu need an infinitive.

ich ... (I ...)	hoffe, ... (hope) versuche, ... (try) beginne / fange an, ... (begin) habe vor, ... (intend) nutze die Chance (use the opportunity)	+ zu + infinitive

Ich hoffe, Deutsch zu studieren.
I hope to study German.

Ich versuche, einen guten Job zu bekommen.
I am trying to get a good job.

- Separable verbs have the zu after the prefix.

Ich habe vor, fernzusehen.
I intend to watch TV.

Relative pronouns

Relative pronouns send the verb to the end of the clause.

They are used to express WHO or THAT or WHICH.

m Der Mann, der im Café sitzt, ist Millionär.
The man who is sitting in the café is a millionaire.

f Die Katze, die unter dem Tisch schläft, ist sehr süß.
The cat that is sleeping under the table is very sweet.

n Das Mädchen, das einen roten Rock trägt, singt in einer Band.
The girl who's wearing a red skirt sings in a band.

Now try this

1 Combine the sentences with **um ... zu ...** .
   (a) Ich fahre nach Italien – ich besuche meine Verwandten.
   (b) Ich gehe ins Sportzentrum – ich nehme 5 Kilo ab.

2 Combine the sentences with **zu**.
   (a) Ich versuche – ich helfe anderen.
   (b) Ich habe vor – ich gehe auf die Uni.

3 Combine the sentences with a relative pronoun.
   (a) Das ist das Geschäft. Das Geschäft hat Sommerschlussverkauf.
   (b) Hier ist eine Kellnerin. Die Kellnerin ist sehr unhöflich.

The answers are also available via the audio link.

The present tense

There are regular and irregular present tense verbs for you here, but look at pages 4 and 5 for the super-irregular verbs haben (to have) and sein (to be).

Present tense regular

Verbs change according to who is doing the action, just like in English: I drink ➡ he drinks.

The present tense describes what is happening now and can be translated 'drink' or 'am drinking'.

machen – to do / to make		
ich	mache	I do / make
du	machst	you do / make
er / sie / es	macht	he / she /it does / makes
wir	machen	we do / make
ihr	macht	you do / make
Sie / sie	machen	they / you do / make

infinitive verb

wir / sie / Sie forms = same as infinitive

- The present tense is used to describe what are you DOING now or what you DO regularly.
- Present tense time expressions include:

  jetzt (now)   heute (today),
  im Moment   dienstags
  (at the moment)   (on Tuesdays).

- You can use the present tense with a time phrase to indicate the FUTURE.

  Morgen fahre ich nach London.
  Tomorrow I am going to London.

Present tense vowel changes

Some verbs have a vowel change in the du and er / sie / es forms of the present tense, but they still have the same endings (-e, -st, -t, etc.).

infinitive verb

geben – to give			
ich	gebe	wir	geben
du	gibst	ihr	gebt
er / sie / es	gibt	Sie / sie	geben

vowel change

nehmen – to take	
ich	nehme
du	nimmst
er / sie / es	nimmt

essen – to eat	
ich	esse
du	isst
er / sie / es	isst

schlafen – to sleep	
ich	schlafe
du	schläfst
er / sie / es	schläft

Sie schläft.

Now try this

Complete the sentences with the correct form of the present tense verb in brackets.

(a) Ich .... gern Musik. (hören)
(b) Meine Schwester .... im eigenen Zimmer. (schlafen)
(c) Ihr .... montags schwimmen, oder? (gehen)
(d) .... du gern Wurst mit Senf? (essen)
(e) Wir .... nie mit dem Auto. (fahren)
(f) Was .... Sie in den Sommerferien? (machen)
(g) .... es eine Ermäßigung für Senioren? (geben)
(h) Mein Bruder .... heute im Bett, weil er krank ist. (bleiben)

More on verbs

To aim for a higher grade, try to include separable and reflexive verbs in your speaking and writing assessments.

Separable verbs

These verbs have two parts: a prefix + the main verb. They go their separate ways when used in a sentence.

← →

Ich sehe oft fern.   I often watch TV.

Ich wasche nicht so gern ab.
I don't much like washing up.

abwaschen	to wash up
aufwachen	to wake up
aussteigen	to get off
einsteigen	to get on
fernsehen	to watch TV
herunterladen	to download
hochladen	to upload
umsteigen	to change (trains, trams, buses)

- Make sure you can use separable verbs in all the tenses.

  PRESENT: Ich steige in Ulm um.
  I change in Ulm.

  PERFECT: Ich bin in Ulm umgestiegen.
  I changed in Ulm.

Separable verbs form the past participle as one word with -ge- sandwiched in the middle: abgewaschen (washed up), ferngesehen (watched TV).

FUTURE: Ich werde in Ulm umsteigen.
I will change in Ulm.

MODALS: Ich muss in Ulm umsteigen.
I have to change in Ulm.

Reflexive verbs

Reflexive verbs need a reflexive pronoun – mich, dich, etc.

sich freuen – to be happy / pleased	
ich freue mich	wir freuen uns
er / sie / es freut sich	ihr freut euch
du freust dich	Sie / sie freuen sich

Note that sich never has a capital letter.
sich freuen auf ... (acc) – to look forward to ...

sich amüsieren	to enjoy oneself
sich entscheiden	to decide
sich erinnern an	to remember
sich langweilen	to be bored
sich interessieren für	to be interested in

Ich interessiere mich für Geschichte.
I am interested in history.

All reflexive verbs use haben in the perfect tense.

Er hat sich rasiert.   He shaved.
Wir haben uns gelangweilt. We were bored.

Now try this

1 Translate the sentences into German.
   (a) I watch TV. I watched TV.
   (b) I change trains at six o'clock. I changed trains at six o'clock.
   (c) I download music. I will download music.
   (d) I washed up. I have to wash up.

2 Complete the sentences with the correct reflexive pronoun.
   (a) Ich erinnere .... kaum an meinen Vater.
   (b) Wir interessieren .... für Mode.
   (c) Habt ihr .... im Jugendklub gelangweilt?
   (d) Hast du .... im Kino amüsiert?

Commands

Use this page to help you give commands and orders accurately.

Sie commands

Swap the present tense round so the verb comes before the pronoun:

Sie hören (you listen) ➡
Hören Sie bitte! Listen!

Schreiben Sie das auf Deutsch auf.
Write that in German.

Geben Sie keine Kontaktdaten an.
Don't give any contact details.

- Separable verbs separate and the prefix goes to the end of the sentence.
  Tauschen Sie nicht Ihre Telefonnummer aus.
  Don't swap your phone number.
- Sein (to be) is irregular.
  Seien Sie nicht aggressiv.
  Don't be aggressive.
- Other words you may come across in commands:

Runter vom Gas!	Reduce your speed!
Gefahr!	Danger!
Warnung!	Warning!
Achtung!	Attention! / Watch out!
Vorsicht!	Be careful!
Verboten!	Forbidden!
Kein Eintritt! ⊖	Keep out!
Nicht betreten!	No entry!
Ausfahrt freihalten!	Keep exit clear!
! Lebensgefahr!	Danger of death!
Privatgrundstück	Private land

Du commands

Use the present tense du form of the verb minus the -st ending.

gehen ➡ du gehst ➡ du gehst ➡ Geh!

Hab viel Spaß.   Have a lot of fun.

Bleib anonym.   Stay anonymous.

Triff niemanden allein.
Don't meet anyone on your own.

Beleidige andere nicht.   Don't insult others.

Such dir einen Spitznamen aus.
Choose a nickname.

> Separable verb – splits!

Some verbs are irregular in the present tense, so make sure you get it right for a command.

essen – to eat   ➡ Iss! – Eat!
fahren – to drive   ➡ Fahr! – Drive!
geben – to give   ➡ Gib her! – Give!
lassen – to leave   ➡ Lass das! – Leave that!
nehmen – to take   ➡ Nimm! – Take!

Now try this

What is this sign asking dog owners to do?

Liebe Hundehalter bitte achten Sie auf ihre Lieblinge und benutzen Sie Grünflächen und Wege nicht als Hundetoilette

Vielen Dank!

Present tense modals

Modal verbs need another verb in the infinitive form, e.g. gehen (to go), kaufen (to buy).
The modal verb comes second in the sentence, while the infinitive is shifted to the very end.

Können (to be able to)

ich / er / sie	kann
du	kannst
sie / wir / Sie	können

Ich kann nicht schwimmen.   I can't swim.

Müssen (to have to / must)

ich / er / sie	muss
du	musst
sie / wir / Sie	müssen

Du musst deine Hausaufgaben machen.
You have to do your homework.

Wollen (to want to)

ich / er / sie	will
du	willst
sie / wir / Sie	wollen

Er will nicht umsteigen.
He doesn't want to change (trains).

Dürfen (to be allowed to)

ich / er / sie	darf
du	darfst
sie / wir / Sie	dürfen

Wir dürfen in die Disko gehen.
We are allowed to go to the disco.

Sollen (to ought to)

ich / er / sie	soll
du	sollst
sie / wir / Sie	sollen

German speakers most often use the
imperfect tense of sollen to express the
sense of 'should'
or 'ought'

Ich sollte meine Großeltern besuchen.
I should visit my grandparents.

Mögen (to like to)

Mögen is rarely used in the present tense
to express liking. Instead, the conditional
form is far more likely to be used in the
sense of 'would like' or 'like'.

ich / er / sie	möchte
du	möchtest
sie / wir / Sie	möchten

Sie möchte Rollschuhlaufen gehen.
She likes to go rollerblading.

The negative form still uses the present
tense form, however:

Ich mag nicht ins Kino gehen.
I don't like to go to the cinema.

Now try this

Write modal sentences using the verbs given in brackets.

(a) Ich gehe um einundzwanzig Uhr ins Bett. (müssen)
(b) In der Schule raucht man nicht. (dürfen)
(c) Du deckst den Tisch. (sollen)
(d) Hilfst du mir zu Hause? (können)
(e) Ich fahre in den Ferien Ski. (wollen)
(f) Ich sehe am Wochenende fern. (mögen)
(g) Meine Freunde fahren mit dem Bus. (müssen)
(h) Ich löse das Problem nicht. (können)

Note that separable verbs come
together as infinitives: ich sehe
fern = fernsehen.

Imperfect modals

Using modals and an infinitive in different tenses is a great way of incorporating a variety of tenses into your work.

Imperfect modals

Infinitive: können – to be able to

Present tense:
ich kann + infinitive at end = I can ... ➡

Imperfect tense:
ich konnte + infinitive at end = I was able to ...

Ich konnte nicht mehr warten.
I couldn't wait any more.

infinitive at the end

The endings change, depending on the subject of the verb.

ich	konnte
du	konntest
er / sie / man	konnte
wir	konnten
Sie / sie	konnten
ihr	konntet

Other modals in the imperfect

- These modals work in the same way as konnte – just add the correct ending.
- There are no umlauts on imperfect tense modals.

müssen	➡	musste	had to
wollen	➡	wollte	wanted to
dürfen	➡	durfte	was allowed to
sollen	➡	sollte	was supposed to
mögen	➡	mochte	liked

Was musstet ihr gestern in Mathe machen?
What did you have to do in maths yesterday?

Er wollte doch nur helfen.
He only wanted to help.

Sie durfte ihn nicht heiraten.
She wasn't allowed to marry him.

Du solltest eine Tablette nehmen.
You should take a pill.

Subjunctive modals (Higher)

Add an umlaut to konnte and mochte and you have the subjunctive. This allows you to talk about things you COULD / WOULD do.

imperfect	➡	subjunctive	
konnte	➡	könnte (could)	+ infinitive
mochte	➡	möchte (would like)	

The subjunctive has the same structure as imperfect modals with the infinitive at the end.

Möchtest du ins Kino gehen?
Would you like to go to the cinema?

Das Schwimmbad könnte geschlossen sein.
The swimming pool could be closed.

Now try this

1 Rewrite these sentences with an imperfect tense modal.
   (a) Ich mache Hausaufgaben. (müssen)
   (b) Sie helfen mir nicht. (können)
   (c) Er kauft eine neue Hose. (wollen)
   (d) Wir räumen das Zimmer auf. (sollen)
   (e) In der Schule kaut man nie Kaugummi. (dürfen)
   (f) Alle Schüler bleiben bis sechzehn Uhr. (müssen)

2 Rewrite these with a subjunctive modal.
   (a) Es wird schwierig. (können)
   (b) Ich fahre nach Berlin. (mögen)

The perfect tense 1

The perfect tense is the main past tense in German. Using it is essential if you are aiming for a top grade.

The perfect tense

- Use the perfect tense to talk about something you have done in the PAST.
- The perfect tense is made up of TWO PARTS:

  the correct form of HABEN or SEIN + past participle at the end.

  Ich habe Musik gehört.
  I listened to music.

Past participles generally start with ge-.

spielen	➡	gespielt (played)
lachen		gelacht (laughed)
fahren	➡	gefahren (drove)

Hast du den Film gesehen? Have you seen the film?

The perfect tense – haben

Most verbs use haben (to have) in the perfect tense:

form of haben + sentence + past participle at the end.

ich habe	
du hast	gekauft (bought)
er / sie / es hat	gemacht (made)
wir haben	besucht (visited)
ihr habt	gesehen (seen)
Sie / sie haben	

Er hat im Reisebüro gearbeitet.
He worked at the travel agency.

Wir haben Frühstück gegessen.
We ate breakfast.

The perfect tense – sein

Some verbs of movement use sein (to be) to make the perfect tense:

form of sein + sentence + past participle at the end.

ich bin	
du bist	gegangen (went)
er / sie / es ist	geflogen (flew)
wir sind	gefahren (drove)
ihr seid	geblieben (stayed)
Sie / sie sind	

Sie ist zu Fuß gegangen.   She went on foot.

Ich bin nach Freiburg gefahren.
I went to Freiburg.

There are some verbs that use **sein** in the perfect tense where there is no apparent movement: **bleiben** is such an example.

Now try this

Write these sentences in the perfect tense.

(a) Ich kaufe eine Jacke.
(b) Wir fliegen nach Portugal.
(c) Ich sehe meinen Freund.
(d) Lena und Hannah gehen in die Stadt.
(e) Ich besuche meine Tante.
(f) Ich bleibe im Hotel.
(g) Was isst du zu Mittag?
(h) Am Samstag hört er Musik.

Put the form of **haben** / **sein** in **second** position and the past participle at the end of the sentence.

The perfect tense 2

Spotting past participles will help you to identify when a text is in the past tense – but watch out for the hidden ge- in separable verbs, such as ferngesehen (watched TV).

Regular past participles

- Begin with ge-.
- End in -t.

Remove -en from the infinitive and replace with –t: machen ➡ macht ➡ gemacht

Das hat ihr Spaß   That was fun
gemacht.   for her.

Some exceptions

Verbs starting with be-, emp- or ver- do not add ge- for the past participle.

Ich habe ...	I ...
besucht	visited
empfohlen	recommended
vergessen	forgot
verloren	lost

Separable verbs add **ge-** between the prefix and the main verb.
hoch**ge**laden uploaded   herunter**ge**laden downloaded

Irregular past participles

There are no rules for forming these past participles – but here are some common ones to learn.

Ich habe ...	gegessen	ate
	getrunken	drank
	genommen	took
	geschlafen	slept
	geschrieben	wrote
	gesungen	sang
	getragen	wore / carried
	getroffen	met
	gestanden	stood
Er ist ...	gerannt	ran
	geschwommen	swam
	gewesen	has been
	gestiegen	climbed
	gestorben	died
	geworden	became

Word order

- The past participle goes at the END of the sentence and the form of haben or sein is in SECOND position.

1 Er   **2** ist   ins Kino   **3** gegangen.
He went to the cinema.

1 Am Montag   **2** habe ich   Fußball   **3** gespielt.
I played football on Monday.

- When the verb has already been sent to the end by a conjunction such as weil (because) or als (when), the part of haben or sein comes AFTER the past participle.

Ich war dankbar, weil er mein Portemonnaie gefunden hat.
I was grateful because he found my purse.

Als er ankam, war er erschöpft.
When he arrived, he was exhausted.

Now try this

Complete the sentences with the correct past participle of the verb in brackets.

(a) Ich habe zu viele Kekse .... (essen)

(b) Haben Sie gut .... ? (schlafen)

(c) Wir haben uns am Bahnhof .... (treffen)

(d) Ich war krank, weil ich den ganzen Tag .... habe. (stehen)

(e) Ich weiß, dass du .... bist. (umsteigen)

(f) Warum hast du die E-Mail .... ? (schreiben)

(g) Ich habe ihr .... , dass sie nicht mitkommen sollte. (empfehlen)

(h) Ich war sehr traurig, als er .... ist. (sterben)

The imperfect tense

You may need to recognise the imperfect tense in reading and listening passages at higher level.

Forming the imperfect tense

- Take the infinitive, e.g. hören (to hear).
- Take off the final -en ➡ hör~~en~~ = hör.
- Add these endings:

ich hörte	I heard / was hearing
du hörtest	you heard / were hearing
er / sie / man hörte	he / she / one heard / was hearing
wir hörten	we heard / were hearing
ihr hörtet	you heard / were hearing
sie / Sie hörten	they / you heard / were hearing

Ich hörte gar nichts.
I didn't hear a thing.

Sie spielten drei Jahre lang mit der Gruppe.
They played for three years with the group.

'To have' and 'to be' in the imperfect

HABEN

ich hatte	I had
du hattest	you had
er / sie / man hatte	he / she / one had
wir hatten	we had
ihr hattet	you had
sie / Sie hatten	they / you had
Ich hatte Glück.	I was lucky.

SEIN

ich war	I was
du warst	you were
er / sie / man war	he / she / one was
wir waren	we were
ihr wart	you were
sie / Sie waren	they / you were
Es war teuer.	It was expensive.

Irregular verbs

- Some verbs have irregular stems in the imperfect tense.
- Add the same basic endings as above to the irregular stems on the right:

  Ich ging – wir gingen (I went – we went)

  Ich fuhr – wir fuhren (I drove – we drove)

Im Stück ging es um eine Beziehung.
The play was about a relationship.

Die Kinder sahen blass aus.
The children looked pale.

Es fand in Hamburg statt.
It took place in Hamburg.

gehen	➡	ging	went
fahren	➡	fuhr	drove
finden	➡	fand	found
kommen	➡	kam	came
nehmen	➡	nahm	took
sehen	➡	sah	saw
sitzen	➡	saß	sat
stehen	➡	stand	stood
tut weh	➡	tat weh	hurt

- Es gab is an impersonal verb and so does not change.

| Es gab ein Haus. | There was a house. |
| Es gab zwei Häuser. | There were two houses. |

Now try this

Translate these imperfect sentences into English.

(a) Sie hatte Angst.

(b) Es war hoffnungslos.

(c) Wo tat es dir weh?

(d) Hörtest du das?

(e) Plötzlich kam uns der Mann entgegen.

(f) Das war eine Überraschung, nicht?

(g) Es war niemand zu Hause.

(h) Sie spielten gern Tischtennis.

The future tense

As well as using the future tense, you can also express future intent using the present tense. Use this page to check you can do both!

Future tense

Use the future tense to talk about things you WILL do or that WILL happen in the future:

form of werden (to become) + sentence + infinitive at the end.

ich werde	
du wirst	vergessen (forget)
er / sie / man wird	spielen (play)
wir werden	holen (collect)
ihr werdet	klopfen (knock)
Sie / sie werden	

Word order in the future tense

Form of werden in second position

① **②** **③** **④**

Nächste Woche werde ich in den Urlaub fahren.

Ich werde erfolgreich sein.
I will be successful.

Wie groß wirst du werden?
How tall will you get?

Morgen wird es kalt sein.
It will be cold tomorrow.

Werden sie auf die Uni gehen?
Will they go to university?

Ich bin froh, dass du zu Besuch kommen wirst.
I am happy that you will come to visit.

Reflexive and separable verbs

- Reflexive verbs – add the pronoun after part of werden:

  Ich werde mich schnell rasieren.
  I will shave quickly.

- Separable verbs – stay together at the end of the sentence:

  Er wird das Lied herunterladen.
  He will download the song.

Present tense with future intent

You can use the present tense to express what you are GOING TO do. Include a time marker to make sure the intent is based in the future.

morgen	tomorrow
übermorgen	the day after tomorrow
nächste Woche	next week

Nächsten Sommer fahren wir nach Amerika.
We are going to America next summer.

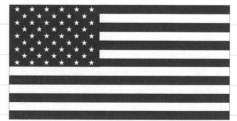

Now try this

Rewrite the sentences in the future tense with 'werden'.

(a) Ich gewinne das Spiel.
(b) Wir gehen in den Freizeitpark.
(c) Sie mieten eine große Wohnung.
(d) Ihr habt große Schwierigkeiten.
(e) Er besteht die Prüfung.
(f) Nächste Woche ziehen wir um.
(g) Schminkst du dich heute?
(h) Ich ziehe mich um sechs Uhr an.

The conditional

The conditional is very similar in structure to the future tense and using it will improve your writing and speaking.

Conditional

Use the conditional to talk about things you WOULD do or that WOULD happen in the future: part of würde (would) + sentence + infinitive at the end.

ich würde	
du würdest	
er / sie / man würde	+ infinitive
wir würden	
ihr würdet	
Sie / sie würden	

Ich würde gern nach Italien fahren.
I would like to go to Italy.

Würden Sie lieber Geschäftsmann oder Klempner werden?
Would you rather become a businessman or a plumber?

Würdest du je rauchen?
Would you ever smoke?

Man würde nie ein Auto kaufen.
One would never buy a car.

würde sein = wäre – would be
würde haben = hätte – would have
es würde geben = es gäbe – there would be

Using wenn

- You often use wenn (if) with the conditional tense.
- Remember: verb – comma – verb!

Wenn ich reich wäre, würde ich keine Designerkleidung kaufen.
If I were rich, I wouldn't buy designer clothes.

Wenn sie ein Vorstellungsgespräch hätte, würde sie rechtzeitig kommen.
If she had an interview, she would arrive on time.

Making requests

Use the conditional tense to make a request for something you WOULD like.

Ich möchte Pommes essen.
I would like to eat chips.

The plural form adds -n.

wir möchten
we would like

sie hätten gern
they would like to have

Sie hätte gern ein neues Handy.
She would like a new mobile.

Now try this

Rewrite these sentences using the conditional.

(a) Ich gehe gern ins Theater.
(b) Er kommt nie zu spät an.
(c) Wir nehmen nie Drogen.
(d) Helfen Sie mir bitte?
(e) Zum Geburtstag bekommt sie am liebsten Geld.
(f) Nächstes Jahr heiraten sie vielleicht.
(g) Wenn Latein Pflicht ist, gehe ich auf eine andere Schule.
(h) Wenn ich das mache, gibt es Krach mit meinen Eltern.

The pluperfect tense

The pluperfect tense is used to say you HAD done something. Use it to aim for a top grade!

Forming the pluperfect

- Use the pluperfect tense to talk about events which HAD happened.
- It is made up from the IMPERFECT of haben or sein + past participle.

ich hatte	
du hattest	Pause gemacht
er / sie / man hatte	(I had had a break)
wir hatten	Freunde gesehen
ihr hattet	(I had seen friends)
sie / Sie hatten	

ich war	
du warst	Ski gefahren
er / sie / man war	(I had been skiing)
wir waren	zu Hause geblieben
ihr wart	(I had stayed at home)
sie / Sie waren	

Haben or sein?

- Some participles take haben and some sein. The same rules apply as for the perfect tense.

Sie hatte kein Wort gesagt.
She had not said a word.

ich hatte	angefangen / begonnen (I had begun)
	gearbeitet (worked)
	gebracht (brought)
	eingeladen (invited)
	erreicht (reached)
	geholt (fetched)
	gelogen (lied)

Er war nicht gekommen.   He had not come.

ich war	geblieben (I had stayed)
	hineingegangen (entered)
	eingeschlafen (fallen asleep)
	vorbeigegangen (gone by)
es war	geschehen (it had happened)

The pluperfect and perfect tenses

Look how similar the pluperfect tense is to the perfect tense.

Ich habe Basketball gespielt.   ➡   Ich hatte Basketball gespielt.
I played basketball.   I had played basketball.

Es hat ihm Spaß gemacht.   ➡   Es hatte ihm Spaß gemacht.
It was fun for him.   It had been fun for him.

Wir sind zur Eishalle gegangen.   ➡   Wir waren zur Eishalle gegangen.
We went to the ice rink.   We had gone to the ice rink.

Now try this

Write these sentences in the pluperfect tense.

(a) Ich habe zu Mittag gegessen.
(b) Sie haben als Stadtführer gearbeitet.
(c) Bist du schwimmen gegangen?
(d) Wir sind in Kontakt geblieben.
(e) Sie sind mit dem Rad in die Stadt gefahren.
(f) Ich habe sie vor einigen Monaten besucht, aber damals war sie schon krank.
(g) Bevor ich ins Haus gegangen bin, habe ich ein Gesicht am Fenster gesehen.
(h) Obwohl ich kaum mit ihm gesprochen habe, schien er sehr freundlich zu sein.

Questions

Knowing how to ask questions as well as answer them is a useful skill in speaking.

Asking questions

You can swap the pronoun and verb round to form a question:

Du hast einen Hund.   You have got a dog.

Hast du einen Hund?   Have you got a dog?

Make sure you use a variety of tenses when you ask questions about events at different times.

Sie sind nach Spanien geflogen.
You flew to Spain.

Sind Sie nach Spanien geflogen?
Did you fly to Spain?

Key question words

Wann?   When?

Warum?   Why?

Was?   What?

Wer?   Who?

Wie?   How?

Wohin?   Where (to)?

Wohin werden Sie in den Urlaub fahren?
Where will you go on holiday?

Wann sind Sie dorthin gefahren?
When did you go there?

Warum hat Ihnen der Film nicht gefallen?
Why didn't you like the film?

Other question words

Was für ...?   What sort of ...?

Was für Bücher lesen Sie gern?   What sort of books do you like reading?

Wie viele?   How many?

Wie viele Stunden pro Woche treiben Sie Sport?
How many hours a week do you do sport?

Wessen?   Whose?

Wessen Idee war das?   Whose idea was that?

Wessen is in the genitive case.

Wen? Wem?   Who(m)?

Wen finden Sie besser?
Who do you find better?

Wen is in the accusative case.

Mit wem spielen Sie Squash?
Who do you play squash with?

Wem is in the dative case after mit.

Using welcher (which)

Welcher agrees with the noun it is asking about.

masc	Welcher Sport? Which sport?
fem	Welche Aufgabe? Which activity?
neut	Welches Fach? Which subject?
pl	Welche Fächer? Which lessons?

Welchen Sport finden Sie am einfachsten?
Which sport do you find the easiest?

Welches Fach machst du am liebsten?
Which subject do you like doing best?

Now try this

1 Turn the sentences into questions.
 (a) Sie lesen gern Science-Fiction-Bücher.
 (b) Sie finden Ihre Arbeit anstrengend.
 (c) Sie möchten nur Teilzeit arbeiten.
 (d) Nächsten Sommer werden Sie nach Australien auswandern.

2 Write questions to ask in your speaking assessment.
 (a) Who is your favourite singer?
 (b) When did you last go to the theatre?
 (c) Why did you become a teacher?
 (d) How often do you eat at a restaurant?
 (e) What sort of shops do you particularly like?

Time markers

Here are some ideas to give a flavour of timing to your work – remember to put the verb in SECOND position if you are starting with one of these time markers.

Present tense

aktuell	current(ly)
heute	today
heutzutage	these days
jetzt	now
normalerweise	normally
seit	since / for

Jetzt, wo ich noch Schülerin bin, muss ich viel lernen.
Now, while I am still a pupil, I must work hard.

Past tenses

gestern	yesterday
vorgestern	the day before yesterday
vor drei Monaten	three months ago
letzte Woche	last week
letztes Wochenende	last weekend
früher	previously
als (kleines) Kind	as a (small) child
neulich	recently

Vor sechs Wochen habe ich mir das Bein gebrochen.
I broke my leg six weeks ago.

Future tense

bald	soon
in Zukunft	in future
morgen (früh)	tomorrow (morning)
übermorgen	day after tomorrow
nächste Woche	next week
am nächsten Tag	on the next day

Wenn ich älter bin, werde ich eine gute Stelle finden.
When I am older, I will find a good job.

General

jeden Tag / täglich	every day / daily
wöchentlich	weekly
eines Tages	one day
immer	always
immer noch	still
schon immer	always
am Anfang	at the start
von Zeit zu Zeit	from time to time
sofort	immediately
rechtzeitig	on time
regelmäßig	regularly

Ich habe schon immer in Wales gewohnt.
I have always lived in Wales.

Now try this

Rewrite these sentences with the time expressions provided in brackets.

(a) Ich spiele Klavier. (seit drei Jahren)
(b) Er hat die Hausaufgaben nicht gemacht. (letzte Woche)
(c) Wir werden in den Bergen wandern gehen. (nächsten Sommer)
(d) Wir wollten das Betriebspraktikum nicht machen. (am Anfang)
(e) Man wird alle Lebensmittel elektronisch kaufen. (in Zukunft)
(f) Ich hoffe, Disneyland zu besuchen. (eines Tages)
(g) Ich hatte Halsschmerzen. (vorgestern)
(h) Sie haben oft Tennis gespielt. (früher)

Numbers

Numbers are really important in a variety of contexts so make sure you know them!

Numbers

1 eins	11 elf	21 einundzwanzig	100 hundert
2 zwei	12 zwölf	22 zweiundzwanzig	101 hunderteins
3 drei	13 dreizehn		200 zweihundert
4 vier	14 vierzehn	*all one word –*	333 dreihundertdreiunddreißig
5 fünf	15 fünfzehn	*however long!*	
6 sechs	16 sechzehn		*no und after dreihundert!*
7 sieben	17 siebzehn	30 dreißig	1000 tausend
8 acht	18 achtzehn	40 vierzig	
9 neun	19 neunzehn	50 fünfzig	
10 zehn	20 zwanzig	60 sechzig	ein Tausend – a thousand
		70 siebzig	eine Million – a million
		80 achtzig	
		90 neunzig	

Ordinal numbers

1st erste	11th elfte		am vierzehnten März	on 14th March
2nd zweite	12th zwölfte		ab dem achten Juni	from 8th June
3rd dritte	13th dreizehnte		vom ersten bis zum dreizehnten Dezember	from 1st to 13th December
4th vierte	14th vierzehnte		nach / vor dem zehnten April	after / before 10th April
5th fünfte				
6th sechste	20th zwanzigste		seit dem dritten Februar	since 3rd February
7th siebte	21st einundzwanzigste			
8th achte	30th dreißigste		YEARS: (im Jahr)	in 1988
9th neunte	31st einunddreißigste		neunzehnhundertachtundachtzig	
10th zehnte			zweitausendzwölf	2012

Now try this

Listen and complete the number gaps.

(a) ☐ 14.– ☐. Mai

(b) ☐ : ☐

(c) € ☐ , ☐

(d) ☐. Januar ☐

(e) € ☐ Millionen

(f) ☐ % Ermäßugung

(g) ☐ : ☐

(h) ☐ Grad

Vocabulary

These pages cover key German vocabulary that you need to know. This section starts with general terms that are useful in a wide variety of situations and then divides into vocabulary for each of the four main topics covered in this revision guide:

1 General vocabulary   **2** Lifestyle   **3** Leisure

4 Home and environment   **5** Work and education

F Sections to be learnt by **all** candidates   **H** Sections to be learnt by Higher candidates only

Learning vocabulary is essential preparation for your reading and listening exams. Don't try to learn too much at once – concentrate on learning and testing yourself on a page at a time.

1 General vocabulary

Comparisons

ähnlich	similar
anders	different
Gegenteil (n)	opposite
gern – lieber – am liebsten	like – prefer – favourite
gleich	equal, same
gut – besser – am besten	good – better – best
hoch – höher – am höchsten	high – higher– highest
im Großen und Ganzen	on the whole
mindest...	the least ...
das ist so ... wie	that's as ... as
so viel ... wie	as much ... as
Unterschied (m)	difference
unterschiedlich	different
vergleichen	to compare
Vergleich (m)	comparison
verschieden	different
viel – mehr – am meisten	many – more – most

Conjunctions

bevor	before
bis	until
damit	so
dass	that
denn	because
entweder ... oder	either ... or
nachdem	after
ob	whether
seit(dem)	since
so dass	so that
sowohl ... als auch	both ... and
während	during
weder ... noch	neither ... nor

Connectives

abgesehen davon	apart from this
als ob	as if, like
also	therefore
angenommen	assumed
außer	except
außerdem	besides
danach	afterwards
dann	then
das heißt (d.h.)	that is (i.e.)
dennoch	nevertheless
deshalb / deswegen	therefore
doch	however, yet
drittens	thirdly
eigentlich	actually
erstens	firstly
jedoch	however
leider	unfortunately
natürlich	naturally
nicht nur ... sondern auch	not just ... but also
ohne Zweifel	doubtless
schließlich	finally
sonst	otherwise
trotzdem	despite
vorausgesetzt dass	given that
zuerst	first
zufällig	accidentally
zweitens	secondly

Prepositions

an	at
auf	on
aus	out of
bei	with, at (house)
durch	through
entlang	along
für	for
gegen	against
gegenüber	opposite
hinter	behind
in	in
mit	with
nach	after
neben	next to
ohne	without
über	over, above
um	around
unter	under
von	from
vor	in front of
vorbei	past
wegen	because of
zu	to
zwischen	between

Negatives

gar nicht	not at all
nicht	not
nicht einmal	not even
nicht mehr	no longer
nie	never
niemals	never
nirgend...	no...
noch nicht	not yet
überhaupt nicht	not at all

Correctness

buchstabieren	to spell
falsch	wrong, false
Fehler (m)	mistake
Recht haben	to be right
richtig	right, correct
Unrecht haben	to be wrong
verbessern	to improve
Verbesserung (f)	correction

Now try this

Pick five words at random from each column and see if you can write a sentence using each word.

General vocabulary

Numbers

Million (f)	million
1. = erste	1st = first
2. = zweite	2nd = second
3. = dritte etc.	3rd = third
Dutzend (n)	dozen
Nummer (f)	number
Paar (n)	pair, couple
Zahl (f)	figure, number
zwo = zwei	two (phone)

Questions

Wann? When?

Warum? Why?

Was für? What sort of?

Was? What?

Wer? Who?

Wessen? Whose?

Wie viel(e)? How much / many?

Wie? How?

Wo? Where?

Wieso? Why?

Woher? From where?

Wohin? Where to?

Key verbs

haben	to have
sein	to be
werden	to become

Greetings and exclamations

Alles Gute!	All the best!
Auf Wiedersehen!	Goodbye!
Bis bald!	See you soon!
Bitte!	You're welcome!
Danke (schön)!	(Many) Thanks!
Entschuldigung!	Excuse me!
Es tut mir leid!	I am sorry!
Frohe Weihnachten!	Happy Christmas!
Gern geschehen!	My pleasure!
Grüß Gott!	Greetings!
Hallo!	Hello!
Herzlich willkommen!	Welcome!
Herzlichen Glückwunsch!	Congratulations!
Mit Vergnügen!	With pleasure!
Schöne Ferien!	Have a good holiday!
Tschüs!	Bye!
Verzeihung!	Pardon!
Viel Glück!	Good luck!
Wie geht es dir / Ihnen?	How are you?

Opinions

Ahnung (f)	inkling, clue
amüsant	amusing
angenehm	pleasant
ängstlich	afraid
ausgezeichnet	excellent
bequem	comfortable
bestimmt	certain(ly)
billig	cheap
dafür	therefore, for it
dagegen	against it
denken	to think
die Nase voll haben	to be fed up
doof	silly
dumm	stupid
ein bisschen	a little, bit
einfach	easy
entsetzlich	dreadful
es kommt darauf an, ob	it depends
satt sein	to be full
fantastisch	fantastic
faszinierend	fascinating
froh	happy
furchtbar	dreadful
gefallen	to please, like
genießen	to enjoy

glauben	to believe
hassen	to hate
herrlich	superb
hervorragend	outstanding
Idee (f)	idea
interessieren (sich für)	to be interested (in)
klasse	great
kompliziert	complicated
können	to be able to
langweilen (sich)	to be bored
langweilig	boring
leicht	easy
lieb	dear, nice
lieben	to love
Farbe (f)	colour
bunt	coloured
hell	light
dunkel	dark
blau	
braun	
gelb	
grau	
grün	
lila	
rosa	
rot	
schwarz	
weiß	

Now try this

Choose ten opinion phrases and write a sentence in German containing each of them.

① General vocabulary

lustig	funny
meinen	to think
Meinung (f)	opinion
mies	lousy
mögen	to like
mühsam	tedious
neu	new
nützlich	useful
nutzlos	useless
praktisch	practical
prima	great
sagen	to say
schade	shame
schlecht	bad
schlimm	bad
schrecklich	awful
schwierig	difficult
sensibel	sensitive
sicher	sure
sogar	even
spitze	awesome
stimmt	correct
teuer	expensive
toll	great
total	totally
typisch	typical
überrascht	surprised
unglaublich	unbelievable
unmöglich	impossible
unsicher	uncertain
vielleicht	perhaps
völlig	completely
vorziehen	to prefer
wahrscheinlich	probably
wichtig	important
wirklich	really
wollen	to want to
wunderbar	wonderful
wunderschön	wonderful
wünschen (sich)	to wish
ziemlich	quite
zustimmen	to agree

The seasons

Jahreszeit (f)	season
Frühling (m)	spring
Sommer (m)	summer
Herbst (m)	autumn
Winter (m)	winter

Days of the week

Woche (f)   week   Tag (m)   day

	Montag Monday	Dienstag Tuesday	Mittwoch Wednesday	Donnerstag Thursday	Freitag Friday	Samstag / Sonnabend Saturday	Sonntag Sunday
07.00							
08.00							

Months

 Januar
 Februar
 März
 April

 Mai
 Juni
 Juli
 August

 September
 Oktober
 November
 Dezember

The clock

fünf nach halb	25 to
fünf vor halb	25 past
genau	exactly
Minute (f)	minute
Mittag (m)	midday
Mitternacht (f)	midnight
nachgehen	to be slow (clock)
pünktlich	punctual
Sekunde (f)	second
spät	late
Stunde (f)	hour
Uhr (f)	clock
Um wie viel Uhr?	What time?
Viertel (n)	quarter
vorgehen	to be fast (clock)
Wie spät ist es?	What's the time?
Zeit (f)	time

Other time expressions

ab	from
ab und zu	now and again
Abend (m)	evening
abends	in the evenings
als	when
Augenblick (m)	moment
bald	soon
damals	then
erst	first
Datum (n)	date
dauern	to last
ehemalig	former
einmal	once
endlich	finally
fast	almost
früh	early
Gegenwart (f)	present
gerade	just, currently
gestern	yesterday
gewöhnlich	usually
heute	today
heutzutage	today
im Voraus	in advance

Now try this

Practise the days of the week and the months of the year by translating the birthdays of ten family members and friends into German.

① General vocabulary

immer	always
inzwischen	meanwhile
Jahrhundert (n)	century
jetzt	now
kürzlich	recent
langsam	slow
letzter/e/es	last
manchmal	sometimes
Moment (m)	moment
montags	on Mondays
Morgen (m)	morning
morgen früh	tomorrow morning
morgens	in the mornings
nachher	afterwards
Nachmittag (m)	afternoon
nächster/e/es	next
Nacht (f)	night
nachts	at night
neulich	recently
noch einmal	once more
normalerweise	normally
nun	now
plötzlich	suddenly
schnell	quick
schon	already
seit	since
selten	rarely
sofort	immediately
täglich	daily
übermorgen	day after tomorrow
Vergangenheit (f)	past
vor Kurzem	recently
vorgestern	day before yesterday
vorher	previously
Vormittag (m)	morning
wieder	again
Wochenende (n)	weekend
Zeitpunkt (m)	moment
zu Ende	at an end
Zukunft (f)	future

Location and distance

außen	outside
außerhalb	beyond
bleiben	to stay
da (drüben)	(over) there
draußen	outside
drinnen	inside
Ecke (f)	corner
entfernt	away
her(aus)	out (of)
herein	in
herum	around
hin(aus)	out (of)
hinein	in
irgendwo	somewhere
liegen	to lie
Mitte (f)	middle
mitten	midway
nah	near
Nähe (f)	proximity
Norden (m)	north
nördlich	northern
oben	above
Ort (m)	place
Osten (m)	east
östlich	eastern
Stadtrand (m)	edge of town
Süden (m)	south
südlich	southern
überall	everywhere
unten	under
vorwärts	forwards
weit	far
Westen (m)	west
westlich	western
Zentimeter (m)	centimetre
zurück	back

auf der linken Seite
on the left

auf der rechten Seite
on the right

links
left

rechts
right

geradeaus
straight on

Weights and measures

alle	all
anderer/e/es	other
beide	both
breit	broad
dick	fat
Ding (n)	thing
Dose (f)	can, tin
Dreieck (n)	triangle
dünn	thin
ein paar	a couple
einige	some
einzeln	individual
enorm	huge
etwa	about

ein Glas
Marmelade

eine Tafel
Schokolade

eine Packung
Chips

eine Flasche
Medizin

eine Scheibe
Toast

eine Dose
Erbsen

Now try this

Cover the English words in the 'Location and distance' section and see how many of the German words you know. Write down the ones you did not know, in German and English, then test yourself again. Keep doing this until you know them all.

① General vocabulary

Flasche (f)	bottle
ganz	quite, whole
genug	enough
gewaltig	vast
Glas (n)	jar, glass
Gramm (n)	gram
groß	big
Größe (f)	size
irgend …	some …
Karton (m)	carton
kaum	hardly
Kilometer (m)	kilometre
klein	small
Kreis (m)	circle
kurz	short
lang	long
leer	empty
Liter (m)	litre
Maß (n)	measure
mehrere	several
Meile (f)	mile
Menge (f)	quantity
messen	to measure
Meter (m)	metre
mindestens	at least
mittel-	medium
mittelgroß	medium
noch	still
nur	only
Quadrat (n)	square
Päckchen (n)	parcel
Packung (f)	package
Paket (n)	packet
Pfund (n)	pound
Rechteck (n)	rectangle
Schachtel (f)	box
Scheibe (f)	slice
Stück (n)	piece
Stückchen (n)	bit
Tube (f)	tube
Tüte (f)	bag
ungefähr	about
viele	many
viereckig	square
voll	full
wenigstens	at least
wiegen	to weigh
Zentimeter (m)	centimetre

Weather

bedeckt	overcast
Blitz (m)	lightning
Donner (m)	thunder
es donnert	it's thundering
feucht	damp
frisch	fresh
Gewitter (n)	thunder storm
Grad (n)	degree
Hagel (m)	hail
heftig	fierce
heiß	hot
heiter	fair, fine and dry
Himmel (m)	sky
kalt	cold
Klima (n)	climate
kühl	cool
Mond (m)	moon
nass	wet
Niederschlag (m)	rainfall
Regen (m)	rain
Schatten (m)	shade
Schauer (m)	shower
Schnee (m)	snow
schneien	to snow
sonnig	sunny
Sturm (m)	storm
stürmisch	stormy
Temperatur (f)	temperature
trocken	dry
warm	warm
Wetter (n)	weather
Wetterbericht (m)	weather report
Wind (m)	wind
windig	windy
Wolke (f)	cloud
wolkig	cloudy

Materials

bestehen aus	to be made of
Baumwolle (f)	cotton
Eisen (n)	iron
Holz (n)	wood
Leder (n)	leather
Metall (n)	metal
Papier (n)	paper
Plastik (n)	plastic
Seide (f)	silk
Silber (n)	silver
Wolle (f)	wool

 die Sonne scheint

 es blitzt

 es regnet

 es friert

 es schneit

 Es ist neblig.

Abbreviations

d.h.	i.e.
DB	German Rail
GmbH	limited company
inkl.	inclusive
Kfz	car
kg	kilogram
km	kilometre
LKW	lorry
MwSt	VAT
PLZ	postcode
usw.	etc.
z.B.	e.g.

Access

besetzt	engaged
Eintritt (m)	entrance
frei	free
geschlossen	closed
offen	open
öffnen	to open
schließen	to close
verboten	forbidden

Now try this

Learn the weather vocabulary above. Then write down in German what the weather has been each day during the past week. Remember to use the past tense.

2 Lifestyle

Health

Abendessen (n)	evening meal
abhängig	addicted
Ader (f)	artery
Aerobics machen	do aerobics
Alkoholiker (m)	alcoholic
alkoholisch	alcoholic
anfangen	to begin
Angst haben	to be afraid
Appetit (m)	appetite
Aprikose (f)	apricot
atmen	to breathe
aufgeben	to give up
aufhören	to stop
backen	to bake
baden	to bathe
Bauch (m)	stomach
Bein (n)	leg
betrunken	drunk
Bewusstsein (n)	consciousness
Bier (n)	beer
Bio-	organic
Blut (n)	blood
Bohne (f)	bean
Braten (m)	roast
brechen	to break
Bratwurst (f)	fried sausage
Brot (n)	bread
Brötchen (n)	bread roll
Butterbrot (n)	sandwich
Chips (pl)	crisps
die Zähne putzen (sich)	to brush your teeth
Droge (f)	drug
Drogenhändler (m)	drug dealer
Drogensüchtige (m/f)	drug addict
Durst (m)	thirst
durstig	thirsty
Ei (n)	egg
einatmen	to breathe in
einnehmen	to take
Eis (n)	ice cream
entspannen (sich)	to relax
Ernährung (f)	diet, nutrition
Erste Hilfe (f)	first aid
Es geht mir gut / schlecht	I am well / unwell.

 Zitrone (f)
 Ananas (f)
 Apfel (m)

Birne (f)

 Erdbeere (f)
 Kirsche (f)
 Pflaume (f)
 Champignon / Pilz (m)

 Kartoffel (f)
 Erbsen (f/pl)
 Blumenkohl (m)
 Paprika (f)

essen	to eat
Essig (m)	vinegar
fallen	to fall
Fett (n)	fat
fettig	fatty
Finger (m)	finger
Fisch (m)	fish
Fleisch (n)	meat
Fruchtsaft (m)	fruit juice
Frühstück (n)	breakfast
frühstücken	to breakfast
fühlen (sich)	to feel
Fuß (m)	foot
Gabel (f)	fork
gebrochen	broken
Gehirn (n)	brain
Gemüse (n)	vegetable
Geruch (m)	smell
Geschmack (m)	taste
(un)gesund	(un)healthy
Gesundheit (f)	health
gewöhnen (sich an)	to get used to
Gewohnheit (f)	habit
glücklich	happy
grillen	to grill
Gurke (f)	cucumber
Haferflocken (pl)	oats
Hähnchen (n)	roast chicken
Hals (m)	neck

halten	to hold, keep
Hand (f)	hand
hart	hard
Herz (n)	heart
Hilfe (f)	help
Himbeere (f)	raspberry
Hunger (m)	hunger
hungrig	hungry
Imbiss (m)	snack
joggen	to jog
Joghurt (m)	yogurt
Kaffee (m)	coffee
Kakao (m)	cocoa
Karotte (f)	carrot
Käse (m)	cheese
Keks (m)	biscuit
Knie (n)	knee
Kopf (m)	head
Körper (m)	body
köstlich	delicious
Kotelett (n)	chop
krank	ill
Krankenhaus (n)	hospital
Krankenwagen (m)	ambulance
Krankheit (f)	illness
Krebs (m)	cancer
Kuchen (m)	cake
lebendig	lively, alive
Lebensmittel (pl)	groceries
Leber (f)	liver

Now try this

Think about what you have eaten and drunk today and yesterday. Check that you can say and write all the items in German.

② Lifestyle

lecker	tasty	sterben	to die	Honig (m)	honey
Löffel (m)	spoon	stressig	stressful	Kalbfleisch (n)	veal
Lunge (f)	lung	Sucht (f)	addiction	Knoblauch (m)	garlic
Magen (m)	stomach	süchtig	addicted	Lachs (m)	salmon
Mahlzeit (f)	meal	Suppe (f)	soup	Mehl (n)	flour
Marmelade (f)	jam	süß	sweet	Nuss (f)	nut
Medikament (n)	medicine	Tabak (m)	tobacco	Pastete (f)	pâté
Messer (n)	knife	Tee (m)	tea	Raucherhusten	smoker's
Milch (f)	milk	Therapie (f)	therapy	(m)	cough
Mineralwasser (n)	mineral water	Thunfisch (m)	tuna	Rauschgift (n)	drug
Mittagessen (n)	lunch	Torte (f)	gateau	Rindfleisch (n)	beef
Mittel (n)	remedy	tot	dead	Rührei (n)	scrambled egg
müde	tired	trainieren	to train	schädlich	harmful
Nahrung (f)	nourishment	trinken	to drink	schmackhaft	tasty
nehmen	to take	übel	sick	Schweinefleisch	pork
nervös	nervous	Unfall (m)	accident	(n)	
Nudeln (pl)	pasta	vegetarisch	vegetarian	Spiegelei (n)	fried egg
Obst (n)	fruit	Vene (f)	vein	Sprudel (m)	sparkling water
Öl (n)	oil	verletzen (sich)	to injure	Stimme (f)	voice
Pfeffer (m)	pepper	Verletzung (f)	injury	Süßigkeit (f)	sweet
Pfirsich (m)	peach	Wasser (n)	water	trimmen (sich)	to keep trim
Pommes (frites)	chips	weh tun	to hurt	Truthahn (m)	turkey
Prost!	Cheers!	weich	soft	Überdosis (f)	overdose
probieren	to try	Wein (m)	wine	übergewichtig	overweight
Pute (f)	turkey	Weintraube (f)	grape	Vollmilch (f)	full-fat milk
rauchen	to smoke	Wurst (f)	sausage	würzig	spicy
Raucher (m)	smoker	Zigarette (f)	cigarette	zunehmen	to put on
Reis (m)	rice	Zucker (m)	sugar		weight
riechen	to smell	Zwiebel (f)	onion		
Rücken (m)	back				
roh	raw			**Relationships and**	
Ruhe (f)	peace			**choices**	
Saft (m)	juice				
Sahne (f)	cream				
Salat (m)	lettuce, salad				
Salz (n)	salt				
satt	full				
scharf	sharp, spicy	abnehmen	to lose weight		
Schinken (m)	ham	Abstinenz (f)	abstinence	allein	alone
schlank	slim	ausruhen (sich)	to relax	alt	old
schlimm	bad	bewegen (sich)	to move	Alter (n)	age
schmecken	to taste	Bewegung (f)	movement	altmodisch	old fashioned
Schmerz (m)	pain	bewusstlos	unconscious	anonym	anonymous
Schmerzen haben	to hurt	Biokost (f)	organic food	Arbeit (f)	job
Schokolade (f)	chocolate	braten	to roast	arbeitslos	unemployed
Schulter (f)	shoulder	Ente (f)	duck	ärgern (sich)	to get annoyed
sniffen	to snort	Entziehungskur (f)	rehab	arm	poor
sollen	should	erbrechen (sich)	to vomit	Armut (f)	poverty
Spinat (m)	spinach	ermüdend	tiring	attraktiv	attractive
sportlich	sporty	fettarm	low-fat	auf die Nerven	to get on your
Spritze (f)	syringe	Forelle (f)	trout	gehen	nerves
spritzen	to inject	Fußgelenk (n)	ankle	Auge (n)	eye
		Gans (f)	goose	ausführen	to take for a
		geräuchert	smoked		walk
		hausgemacht	homemade	auskommen mit	to get on with
				Ausländer (m)	foreigner

Now try this

To help you learn food vocabulary, write out the German words in two lists – foods that you like and foods that you don't like. Then memorise all the foods from each list.

② Lifestyle

aussehen	to look	Freiwillige (m/f)	volunteer	(keine) Aussicht	to have (no)
aussetzen	to abandon	Freund (m)	friend	auf Arbeit haben	hope of
Ausweis (m)	identification	Freundschaft (f)	friendship		work
Bart (m)	beard	füttern	to feed (animal)	Kind (n)	child
bedürftig	needy	Gast (m)	guest	komisch	funny, curious
beitragen zu	to contribute to	Gastfreundschaft	hospitality	Kriminalität (f)	criminality
benachteiligen	to disadvantage	(f)		kritisieren	to criticise
berühmt	famous	Gastgeber (m)	host	kümmern (sich um)	to care (for)
Besuch (m)	visit	geboren	born	Kuss (m)	kiss
besuchen	to visit	Geburt (f)	birth	küssen	to kiss
bevorzugen	to prefer	Geburtsdatum (n)	date of birth	Laune (f)	mood
bitten	to ask	Geburtsort (m)	place of birth	lebhaft	lively
blöd	stupid	Geburtstag (m)	birthday	ledig	unmarried
Blödsinn (m)	nonsense	Gefühl (n)	feeling	Leute (pl)	people
böse	angry	gemein	mean	lockig	curly
Brieffreund (m)	penfriend	geschieden	divorced	Mädchen (n)	girl
Brille (f)	glasses	Geschwister (pl)	siblings	Mann (m)	man
bringen	to bring	Gesellschaft (f)	society	mitmachen	to join in
Bruder (m)	brother	Gesicht (n)	face	multikulturell	multicultural
Cousin/e (m/f)	cousin	getrennt	separated	Mund (m)	mouth
Dame (f)	lady	Gewalt (f)	violence	Mutti / Mutter (f)	mum / mother
danken	to thank	glatt	straight	Nase (f)	nose
Dieb (m)	thief	Gleichheit (f)	equality	nennen	to name
dürfen	to be allowed to	großartig	splendid	nerven	to annoy
egoistisch	egotistic	Großeltern (pl)	grandparents	nett	nice
ehrlich	honest	Grund (m)	reason	(nicht) leiden	(not) to
einladen	to invite	gut / schlecht	in a good / bad	können	tolerate
Einladung (f)	invitation	gelaunt	mood		
einsam	lonely	gute / schlechte	to be in a	Goldfisch (m)	
einverstanden	agreed	Laune haben	good / bad		
Einwanderer (m/f)	immigrant		mood		
Einzelkind (n)	only child	Haar (n)	hair		
Eltern (pl)	parents	Halb-	half-	Hund (m)	
entschuldigen	to apologise	hässlich	ugly		
(sich)		Hausnummer (f)	house number		
erfahren	experienced	Haustier (n)	pet	Kaninchen (n)	
erfüllen	to fulfil	Hautfarbe (f)	skin colour		
erlauben	to allow	Heim (n)	home		
erleben	to experience	Heimleiter (m)	warden		
ernst	serious	Heimleitung (f)	management	Katze (f)	
Erwachsene (m/f)	adult	heiraten	to marry		
Familie (f)	family	heißen	to be called		
Familienmitglied	family member	herrisch	domineering	Pferd (n)	
(n)		hilfsbereit	helpful		
Familienname (m)	surname	hoffen	to hope		
Feier (f)	party	hübsch	pretty		
feiern	to celebrate	humorlos	humourless	Maus (f)	
Fest (n)	party, festival	humorvoll	humourous		
Frau (f)	woman, Mrs	jung	young		
frech	cheeky	Käfig (m)	cage		
freiwillig	voluntarily			Meerschweinchen	
				(n)	
				Vogel (m)	

② Lifestyle

niemand	nobody
Not (f)	hardship
obdachlos	homeless
Ohr (n)	ear
Oma (f)	granny
Opa (m)	grandpa
Onkel (m)	uncle
optimistisch	optimistic
Persönlichkeit (f)	personality
pessimistisch	pessimistic
Postleitzahl (f)	postcode
Rasse (f)	race
Rassismus (m)	racism
rassistisch	racist
reich	rich
Reisepass (m)	passport
Rentner (m)	pensioner
sauer	cross
schämen (sich)	to be ashamed
scheiden (sich lassen)	to get divorced
Schnurrbart (m)	moustache
schön	lovely, beautiful
schüchtern	shy
Schwager (m)	brother-in-law
schwatzen	to chat
Schwester (f)	sister
Schwieger-	-in-law
selbst	(my / your)self
Sohn (m)	son
sorgen für	to care for
spenden	to donate
stehlen	to steal
Stief-	step-
still	quiet
Straße (f)	street
Streit (m)	argument
streiten (sich)	to argue
Tante (f)	aunt
Tier (n)	animal
Tochter (f)	daughter
traurig	sad
Trauring (m)	wedding ring
trennen (sich)	to separate
Typ (m)	guy, bloke
Umfrage (f)	survey
(un)freundlich	(un)friendly
(un)geduldig	(im)patient

(un)höflich	(im)polite
(un)ordentlich	(un)tidy
(un)sympathisch	(un)likeable
unternehmungs-lustig	adventurous
unterstützen	to support
(un)zufrieden	(dis)satisfied
Vandalismus (m)	vandalism
Vati / Vater (m)	dad / father
Verbrechen (n)	crime
vergeben	to forgive
Verhältnis (n)	relationship
verheiratet	married
verloben (sich)	to get engaged
verlobt	engaged
verstehen (sich mit)	to get on (with)
Vogel (m)	bird
Vorliebe (f)	preference
Vorname (m)	first name
vorstellen (sich)	to introduce
wachsen	to grow
wegen	concerning
weinen	to cry
Wellensittich (m)	budgerigar
witzig	funny
Wohltätigkeit (f)	charity
Wohnort (m)	residence
Zahn (m)	tooth
Zeug (n)	stuff
Zuhause (n)	home
Zwillinge (pl)	twins

adoptiert	adopted
ähnlich	similar
Alleinerziehende	single parent
alleinstehend	single
angeberisch	pretentious
Anschrift (f)	address
auf Grund	due to
ausgeglichen	balanced
Bedürftige (m/f)	person in need
Begegnung (f)	encounter
begehen	to commit
Bekannte (m/f)	acquaintance

Beziehung (f)	relationship
Braut (f)	bride
Bräutigam (m)	groom
deprimiert	depressed
ehrenamtlich	voluntary
eifersüchtig	jealous
eingebildet	smug
Eingliederung (f)	integration
Enkel (m)	grandson
Enkelin (f)	granddaughter
Geschlecht (n)	gender, sex
Gewalttätigkeit (f)	violence
großzügig	generous
Humor (m)	humour
in Form sein	to be in shape
Junggeselle (m)	bachelor
Kanarienvogel (m)	canary
Karriere (f)	career
leiden	to suffer
magersüchtig	anorexic
minderjährig	under-age
Mindesthaltbar-keitsdatum (n)	sell-by date
miteinander	together
Neffe (m)	nephew
Nichte (f)	niece
Papagei (m)	parrot
Pensionär/in (m/f)	pensioner
Rassenvorurteile (pl)	racial prejudice
Rassist (m)	racist
Schildkröte (f)	tortoise
selbstständig	independent
selbstbewusst	self-confident
Staatsangehörig-keit (f)	nationality
Straftat (f)	offence
Trauung (f)	marriage
treu	true, faithful
Verlobte (m/f)	fiancé
vermeiden	to avoid
verrückt	crazy, mad
Verwandte (m/f)	relative
verzeihen	to forgive
Vetter (m)	cousin
volljährig	of legal age
Vorwahl (f)	code (phone)
zuverlässig	reliable

Now try this

Make two lists in German – male and female – of all the words for family members you can think of, using this section to help you. Learn your words in pairs – male with female – and see how many you can remember after two minutes.

③ Leisure

Free time and media

Abenteuerfilm (m)	adventure film
Abteilung (f)	department
akzeptieren	to accept
altmodisch	old-fashioned
amüsieren (sich)	to amuse
anbieten	to offer
Anfang (m)	beginning
Angebot (n)	offer
angeln	to fish
anprobieren	to try on
Anzug (m)	suit
Apotheke (f)	pharmacy
Armband (n)	bracelet
aufnehmen	to record
aufregend	exciting
Ausflug (m)	outing
Ausgang (m)	exit
ausgeben	to spend
ausgehen	to go out
ausverkauft	sold out
Auswahl (f)	selection
Automat (m)	vending machine
Bäckerei (f)	baker's
Badeanzug (m)	swimming costume
Badehose (f)	trunks
Bargeld (n)	cash
Benutzer (m)	user
berühren	to touch
beschweren (sich)	to complain
besonders	particularly
BH (m)	bra
Blumenladen (m)	florist
Bluse (f)	blouse
brauchen	to need
Brieftasche (f)	wallet
Buch (n)	book
Buchhandlung (f)	bookshop
Chatroom (m)	chatroom
chatten	to chat (online)
Drogerie (f)	chemist
drücken	to press
Ecke (f)	corner
10-Euro-Schein (m)	10-euro note
2-Euro-Stück (n)	2-euro coin

 Gürtel (m)

 Hemd (n)

 Hut (m)

 Kleid (n)

 Krawatte (f) / Schlips (m)

 Rock (m)

 Schal (m)

 Schuh (m)

 Socke (f)

Eingang (m)	entrance
(ein)kaufen	to buy
Einkaufskorb (m)	shopping basket
Einkaufstasche (f)	shopping bag
Einkaufszentrum (n)	shopping centre
einpacken	to pack
Eintrittskarte (f)	ticket
Eintrittsgeld (n)	admission fee
Eislaufen (n)	ice skating
Elektrogeschäft (n)	electrical shop
Empfänger (m)	recipient
eng	narrow
erzählen	to tell
es passt / steht dir	it fits / suits you
Fahrstuhl (m)	lift
Feierabend (m)	evening off
fernsehen	to watch TV
Fischgeschäft (n)	fishmonger
Fitnesszentrum (n)	gym
Fleischerei (f)	butcher
Fotoapparat (m)	camera
Freibad (n)	outside pool
Freizeit (f)	freetime
Friseur(salon) (m)	hairdresser
funktionieren	to work, function
Fußball (m)	football
geben	to give
gehen	to walk, go
Geld (n)	money
Geschäft (n)	shop
gestreift	striped
gewinnen	to win
Gitarre (f)	guitar
gratis	free
Gruppe (f)	group, band
günstig	cheap
Hallenbad (n)	indoor pool
Halskette (f)	necklace
Handschuh (m)	glove
Handtasche (f)	handbag
Hausschuh (m)	slipper
herunterladen	to download
hochladen	to upload
holen	to fetch
hören	to hear
Hose (f)	trousers
Jacke (f)	jacket
kaputt	broken
Kasse (f)	till

Now try this

Look at the clothes that you and your friends are wearing today. Check that you can write and say them all in German.

③ Leisure

German	English	German	English	German	English
Kaufhaus (n)	department store	Ohrring (m)	earring	speichern	to store
kegeln	to bowl	Pfund (n)	pound	Spiel (n)	game
Kino (n)	cinema	Portemonnaie (n)	purse	spielen	to play
Klamotten (pl)	clothes	Preis (m)	price	Spielzeug (n)	toy
Klarinette (f)	clarinet	Pulli (m)	jumper	Spitzname (m)	nickname
Klavier (n)	piano	Quantität (f)	quantity	Sport treiben	to do sport
Kleidung (f)	clothes	Quittung (f)	receipt	Stadion (n)	stadium
Kleingeld (n)	change	Rabatt (m)	discount	Star (m)	celebrity
klettern	to climb	Rad fahren	to cycle	Stiefel (m)	boot
Komikheft (n)	comic	raten	to advise	Strumpfhose (f)	tights
Konditorei (f)	cake shop	reduziert	reduced	Tasche (f)	bag
Konzert (n)	concert	Regenmantel (m)	raincoat	Taschengeld (n)	pocket money
kosten	to cost, taste	Regenschirm (m)	umbrella	Tätowierung (f)	tattoo
kostenlos	free	Reinigung (f)	cleaner's	Tischtennis (n)	table tennis
Kostüm (n)	costume	reiten	to ride	Ton (m)	sound
Krimi (m)	thriller	rennen	to run	Tor (n)	goal
Kunde (m)	customer	Rest (m)	remainder	Trainingsanzug (m)	tracksuit
Kunstgalerie (f)	art gallery	Risiko (n)	risk	treffen (sich mit)	to meet
Künstler (m)	artist	Rollschuh laufen	to rollerskate	Trompete (f)	trumpet
lachen	to laugh	Rolltreppe (f)	escalator	turnen	to do gymnastics
Laden (m)	shop	romantisch	romantic		
Ladenbesitzer (m)	shop owner	Ruhetag (m)	rest day	überwachen	to supervise
laufen	to run	sammeln	to collect	Umkleidekabine (f)	changing room
lehrreich	educational	Sammlung (f)	collection	Unterhaltung (f)	entertainment
lesen	to read	Sänger (m)	singer	Unterhose (f)	underpants
Liebesfilm (m)	love film	schaffen	to create	Verein (m)	club, society
Lieblings-	favourite-	Schaufenster (n)	shop window	verlieren	to lose
Lied (n)	song	schick	smart	Volksmusik (f)	folk music
liefern	to deliver	schießen	to shoot	vorschlagen	to suggest
Liste (f)	list	Schlafanzug (m)	pyjamas	Vorstellung (f)	performance
Lust (f)	desire	Schlange stehen	to queue	Vorteil (m)	advantage
mähen	to mow	Schlittschuh laufen	to ice skate	wählen	to choose
Mantel (m)	coat	schminken (sich)	to put on make-up	Wahrheit (f)	truth
Marke (f)	brand			wandern	to hike
Markt (m)	market	Schmuck (m)	jewellery	Warenhaus (n)	warehouse
Maus (f)	mouse	Schwimmbad (n)	swimming pool	warten	to wait
Metzgerei (f)	butcher	schwimmen	to swim	Wäscherei (f)	laundry
Mitglied (n)	member	Segelboot (n)	sailing boat	Waschsalon (m)	launderette
mitgehen / kommen	to accompany	segeln	to sail	wechseln	to change
		sehen	to see	Werbung (f)	advertisement
Mode (f)	fashion	Seifenoper (f)	soap opera	werfen	to throw
modisch	fashionable	Sendung (f)	programme	wissen	to know
Mütze (f)	cap, beanie	umziehen (sich)	to change	Zeichentrickfilm (m)	cartoon
nach Haus(e)	home	Slip (m)	briefs		
Nachrichten (pl)	news	Sonderangebot (n)	special offer	Zeitschrift (f)	magazine
Nachteil (m)	disadvantage			Zeitung (f)	newspaper
Nachthemd (n)	nightshirt	Sparkasse (f)	savings bank	zerbrechlich	delicate
Notausgang (m)	emergency exit	sparsam	economical	ziehen	to pull
		Spaß machen	to be fun	zurücklassen	to leave
Nutzen (m)	use	spazieren gehen	to go for a walk	zusammen	together
				Zuschauer (m)	spectator

Now try this

Pick a letter of the alphabet and copy the German words beginning with that letter from this page. Then close the book and see if you can add the English words beside them. Check and repeat with another letter when they are all correct.

③ Leisure

H HIGHER

Andenken (n)	souvenir
annehmen	to accept
Anprobe (f)	fitting
begleiten	to accompany
Bergsteigen (n)	mountaineering
Betriebsferien (pl)	company holiday
entdecken	to discover
Etikett (n)	label
fertig werden mit	to manage
Geige (f)	violin
gelangweilt	bored
herabgesetzt	reduced
Leichtathletik (f)	athetics
Möbelgeschäft (n)	furniture store
Pantoffel (m)	slipper
pleite	broke, skint
preiswert	cheap
Schauspiel (n)	play
Sommer- / Winter-schlussverkauf (m)	summer / winter sale
Strickjacke (f)	cardigan
Überraschung (f)	surprise
umsonst	free
Untertitel (m)	subtitle
Vergnügen (n)	pleasure
wirtschaftlich	economic
zweifeln	to doubt

Holidays

F FOUNDATION

abfahren	to depart
abholen	to fetch
Afrika	Africa
Alpen (pl)	the alps
ankommen	to arrive
Ärmelkanal (m)	English Channel
Asien	Asia
Auskunft (f)	information
aussteigen	to get out
Autovermietung (f)	car rental
Badetuch (n)	towel
Bahnsteig (m)	platform
bedienen	to serve

Bedienung (f)	service
Belgien	Belgium
beliebt	popular
besichtigen	to visit
bestellen	to order
bezahlen	to pay
bleiben	to stay
Bockwurst (f)	sausage
Boot (n)	boat
Brauch (m)	need
Broschüre (f)	brochure
Burg (f)	castle
Dampfer (m)	steamboat
Dänemark	Denmark
Donau (f)	Danube
direkt	direct
einsteigen	to get on
entwerten	to validate
erinnern (sich)	to remember
Ermäßigung (f)	discount
Europa	Europe
Fähre (f)	ferry
fahren	to drive, go
Fahrpreis (m)	ticket price
Fahrradverleih (m)	bike hire
Fahrt (f)	journey
Fasching (m)	carnival
Flughafen (m)	airport
Flugzeug (n)	airplane
folgen	to follow
fotografieren	to photograph
Freizeitpark (m)	theme park
Frikadelle (f)	meatball
führen	to lead
Führerschein (m)	driving licence
Gasthaus (n)	B & B
gemischt	mixed
Getränk (n)	drink
Gleis (n)	platform
Griechenland	Greece
Hauptgericht (n)	main course
Helm (m)	home
Kellner (m)	waiter
herumfahren	to drive round
Imbissstube (f)	snack bar
Indien	India
Jugendherberge (f)	youth hostel
Kännchen (n)	pot
Koffer (m)	suitcase
Köln	Cologne

Kreuzung (f)	crossing
Kunstwerk (n)	artwork
Küste (f)	coast
Land (n)	country
Landschaft (f)	landscape
Linie (f)	line
Meer (n)	sea
Mittelmeer (n)	Mediterranean
Motor (m)	engine
Motorrad (n)	motorbike
München	Munich
Nachspeise (f)	dessert
Nachtisch (m)	dessert
die Niederlande (pl)	Netherlands
Nordsee (f)	North Sea

Deutschland	
die Schweiz	
die Türkei	
die Vereinigten Staaten	
England	
Frankreich	
Großbritannien	
Irland	
Italien	
Österreich	
Schottland	
Spanien	
Wales	

Now try this

Highlight all the words for countries in this section. Learn them, then close the book and see how many you can write from memory. Learn again those you got wrong, then test yourself again.

③ Leisure

Öffnungszeiten (pl)	opening times	Silvester	New Year's Eve	Weg (m)	way
örtlich	local	simsen	to text	weggehen	to go away
Ostern	Easter	Ski fahren	to ski	Weihnachten	Christmas
Ostsee (f)	Baltic Sea	sonnen (sich)	to sunbathe	weiterfahren	to drive on
Panne (f)	breakdown	Sonnencreme (f)	suncream	Wien	Vienna
Pension (f)	guesthouse	Sonnenschirm (m)	sunshade	windsurfen	to windsurf
Pfingsten	Whitsun	sonst nichts	nothing else	Wohnwagen (m)	caravan
Polen	Poland	Speisekarte (f)	menu	zahlen	to pay
Portion (f)	portion	Speisesaal (m)	dining room	Zahnbürste (f)	toothbrush
Rechnung (f)	bill	Speisewagen (m)	dining car	Zahnpasta (f)	toothpaste
Reise (f)	journey	Spezialität (f)	speciality	Zelt (n)	tent
Reisebüro (n)	travel agency	Stadtbummel (m)	city wander	zelten	to camp
Reisebus (m)	coach	Stadtführung (f)	city tour	Zug (m)	train
reisen	to travel	Stau (m)	traffic jam	zum ermäßigten	at a reduced
Reisende (m/f)	traveller	Stehcafé (n)	café bar	Preis	price
Reisepass (m)	passport	Strand (m)	beach	zurückfahren	to drive back
Reisetasche (f)	holdall	Straßenkarte (f)	road map	zurückgehen	to go back
Reiseziel (n)	destination	suchen	to look for	Zweibettzimmer	double room
reservieren	to reserve	surfen	to surf	(n)	
Reservierung (f)	reservation	Tagesgericht (n)	day's dish	zweiter Klasse	second class
Rezeption (f)	reception	Tagesmenü (n)	daily menu		
Richtung (f)	direction	tanken	to fill tank		
Rucksack (m)	rucksack	Tankstelle (f)	petrol station		
Rundfahrt (f)	round trip	tanzen	to dance		
Russland	Russia	Tanzen (n)	dance		
Schaschlik (n)	kebab	Tourismus (m)	tourism		
Schiff (n)	ship	Touristen-	tourist		
Schlafraum (m)	dormitory	information (f)	information	Anmeldung (f)	signing in
Schlafsack (m)	sleeping bag	Trinkgeld (n)	tip	Aufenthalt (m)	stay
Schlafwagen (m)	sleeping car	Türkei	Turkey	beeilen (sich)	to hurry
Schließfach (n)	locker	Überfahrt (f)	crossing	bestätigen	to confirm
Schloss (n)	castle	übernachten	to spend the	Bodensee (m)	Lake
Schnellimbiss (m)	snack bar		night		Constance
See (f)	sea	Übernachtung (f)	overnight stay	Eilzug (m)	express train
See (m)	lake	überqueren	to cross	Erlebnis (n)	experience
seekrank	seasick	umsteigen	to change	Fremdenzimmer	guest room
sehenswert	worth seeing	Unterkunft (f)	accommodation	(n)	
Sehenswürdig-	sights	unterwegs	en route	Gebirge (n)	mountains
keiten (pl)		Urlaub (m)	holiday	Genf	Geneva
Seife (f)	soap	verbringen	to spend time	Hausordnung (f)	house rules
Selbstbedienung	self-service	verpassen	to miss	Klimaanlage (f)	air
(f)		verspäten (sich)	to be delayed		conditioning
Senf (m)	mustard	Verspätung (f)	delay	Meeresfrüchte	seafood
Sonnenbrand (m)	sunburn	Vollpension (f)	full-board	(f/pl)	
Sonnenbrille (f)	sunglasses	Vorspeise (f)	starter	Nahverkehrszug	commuter
servieren	to serve	Wagen (m)	car	(m)	train
Serviette (f)	serviette	Wartesaal (m)	waiting room	Rückfahrkarte (f)	return ticket
Sicherheitsgurt	seatbelt			unterbringen	to house
(m)				Verbindung (f)	connection
				Zoll (m)	toll
				Zuschlag (m)	supplement

⊢┼⊣	⟶○	🛁	🖼	🚿
Fitnessraum (m)	Schlüssel (m)	mit Bad	mit Blick auf	mit Dusche
gym	key	with a bath	with a view of	with a shower

Now try this

Highlight 10–15 words on this page which could be used to describe a recent holiday you have had. Write sentences in German using each of them.

4 Home and environment

Home and local area

-einrichtungen	facilities
-möglichkeiten	possibilities
Ampel (f)	traffic lights
(an)klopfen	to knock
anziehen	to put on
anziehen (sich)	to dress
Apparat (m)	device
Arbeitszimmer (n)	study
aufstehen	to get up
Ausfahrt (f)	road exit
ausmachen	to turn off
Aussicht (f)	view
Autobahn (f)	motorway
babysitten	to babysit
Bad (n)	bath
Badewanne (f)	bath tub
Badezimmer (n)	bathroom
Bahnhof (m)	station
Balkon (m)	balcony
Bauernhaus (n)	farmhouse
Bauernhof (m)	farm
Berg (m)	mountain
Besteck (n)	cutlery
betreten	to enter
Bett (n)	bed
Betttuch (n)	sheet
Bild (n)	picture
Blick (m)	look
Boden (m)	floor
Brücke (f)	bridge
Brunnen (m)	fountain
Bücherei (f)	library
Bücherregal (n)	bookshelf
Bürgersteig (m)	pavement
Busbahnhof (m)	bus terminal
Dach (n)	roof
Decke (f)	blanket
decken	to lay
Denkmal (n)	monument
Diele (f)	hall
Dom (m)	cathedral
Doppelhaus (n)	semi-detached house

Dorf (n)	village
Dusche (f)	shower
eigen	own
Einbahnstraße (f)	one way street
Einfahrt (f)	driveway
Einfamilienhaus (n)	detached house
Einwohner (m)	inhabitant
elektrisch	electric
Elektroherd (m)	electric oven
Erdgeschoss (n)	ground floor
Essecke (f)	dining corner
Esszimmer (n)	dining room
Etage (f)	floor
Etagenbett (n)	bunkbed
Fabrik (f)	factory
Fahrschein (m)	ticket
Feiertag (m)	holiday
Fenster (n)	window
Fernsehen (n)	television
Fernseher (m)	television
flach	flat
Flur (m)	hall
freuen (sich auf)	to look forward to
freuen (sich über)	to be pleased about
Fußgängerzone (f)	pedestrian zone
Garage (f)	garage
Garten (m)	garden
Gebäude (n)	building
Gegend (f)	area
Gerät (n)	appliance
Geschenk (n)	present
Geschirr (n)	crockery
Gras (n)	grass
gratulieren	to congratulate
Grill (m)	barbecue, grill
Hafen (m)	harbour
Haltestelle (f)	stop
Hauptbahnhof (m)	main station
Hauptstadt (f)	capital city
Haus (n)	house
Haushalt (m)	household
Hecke (f)	hedge

helfen	to help
Herd (m)	oven
historisch	historic
Hochhaus (n)	highrise
Hochzeit (f)	wedding
Industrie (f)	industry
industriell	industrial
Insel (f)	island
Jugendklub (m)	youth club
Kanal (m)	canal
Karte (f)	map, ticket
Keller (m)	cellar
Kirche (f)	church
Kirchturm (m)	church tower
Kleiderschrank (m)	wardrobe
klingeln	to ring
kochen	to cook
Kommode (f)	dresser
Kopfkissen (n)	pillow
Küche (f)	kitchen
Kühlschrank (m)	fridge
Lampe (f)	lamp
Landkarte (f)	map
leben	to live
Leben (n)	life
leeren	to empty
legen	to put
Leiter (f)	ladder
Licht (n)	light
Lokal (n)	pub
machen	to make
Marktplatz (m)	market place
Mauer (f)	outside wall
Mehrzweckraum (m)	multi-purpose room
Miete (f)	rent
mieten	to rent
Mikrowelle (f)	microwave
Möbel (n)	furniture
möbliert	furnished
Nachbar (m)	neighbour
nach Hause	to home
nach oben	to the top
nach unten	to the bottom
Nachttisch (m)	bedside table
Natur (f)	nature
Ofen (m)	oven

Autobahn (f)

Bäume (mpl)

Berge (mpl)

Gebäude (npl)

Fabrik (f)

Weise (f)

Now try this

Write down all the verbs from this page. See how many of them you know already and then see how long it takes you to remember all their meanings in English.

④ Home and environment

Ordnung (f)	order	Tasse (f)	cup
Parkplatz (m)	parking space	Taufe (f)	baptism
Plakat (n)	poster	Tiefkühlschrank (m)	freezer
Platz (m)	place, square	Tisch (m)	table
Post (f)	post office	Tischdecke (f)	tea towel
putzen	to clean	Tischtuch (n)	tablecloth
Rasen (m)	lawn	Toilette (f)	toilet
Rathaus (n)	town hall	Toilettenpapier (n)	toilet paper
Regal (n)	shelf	Topf (m)	saucepan
Reihenhaus (n)	terrace	Traum (m)	dream
Rezept (n)	recipe	Treppe (f)	stair
Sache (f)	thing	Treppenhaus (n)	stairway
Sackgasse (f)	cul-de-sac	tun	to do
S-Bahn (f)	suburban train	Tür (f)	door
schenken	to give	Turm (m)	tower
schlafen	to sleep	U-Bahn (f)	underground
Schlafzimmer (n)	bedroom	umgeben von	surrounded by
Schlüssel (m)	key	umziehen	to move house
Schrank (m)	cupboard		
Schreibtisch (m)	desk	Umgebung (f)	surroundings
Schublade (f)	drawer	verlassen	to leave
Sessel (m)	armchair	vorbereiten	to prepare
setzen (sich)	to sit down	Vorhang (m)	curtain
Sitz (m)	seat	Vorort (m)	suburb
Spiegel (m)	mirror	Wald (m)	wood, forest
Spielplatz (m)	playground	Wand (f)	wall
Sportzentrum (n)	sports centre	Waschbecken (n)	basin
Spüle (f)	sink	Waschküche (f)	laundry room
Spülmaschine (f)	dishwasher	Waschmaschine (f)	washing machine
Stadt (f)	town		
Stadtmitte (f)	town centre	Wiese (f)	meadow
Stadtplan (m)	town map	Wohnblock (m)	block of flats
Stadtrand (m)	edge of town	wohnen	to live
Stadtteil (m)	district	Wohnung (f)	flat
Stadtviertel (n)	district	Wohnzimmer (n)	sitting room
Stadtzentrum (n)	town centre	Zebrastreifen (m)	zebra crossing
stattfinden	to take place		
stecken	to put	zeigen	to show
stellen	to put	Zentralheizung (f)	central heating
Stereoanlage (f)	hi-fi		
Stock (m)	floor	Zentrum (n)	centre
Stockwerk (n)	storey	Zimmer (n)	room
Straße (f)	street	zu Hause	at home
Straßenbahn (f)	tram	zurückkommen	to come back
Strom (m)	power		
Stuhl (m)	chair		

HIGHER H

Abstellraum (m)	store room
aufpassen auf	to look after
ausschalten	tu turn off
beeilen (sich)	to hurry
Dachboden (m)	attic
Eigentumswohnung (f)	freehold flat
einschalten	to turn on
Feuerwerk (n)	firework
gemütlich	cosy
Grünanlage (f)	park
geräumig	spacious
Heiligabend	Christmas Eve
Mietwohnung (f)	rented flat
Namenstag (m)	namesday
öffentliche Verkehrsmittel (pl)	public transport
Postamt (n)	post office
Rollladen (m)	roller blind
Umzug (m)	procession
Verkehrsamt (n)	tourist office
Wintergarten (m)	conservatory
Zaun (m)	fence

Bahnhof (m)

Bibliothek (f)

Dom (m)

Einkaufszentrum (n)

Kino (n)

Kirche (n)

Fitnesszentrum (n)

Rathaus (n)

Spielplatz (m)

Now try this

Break your vocabulary learning into manageable chunks. For example, choose all the S words on this page to learn, either by covering up the English words, making learning cards or asking a friend to test you.

④ Home and environment

Environment

Abfall (m)	rubbish
Abfalleimer (m)	rubbish bin
Abgase (pl)	emissions
Altpapier (n)	scrap paper
anbauen	to extend
Batterie (f)	battery
bedrohen	to threaten
Benzin (n)	petrol
biologisch	organic
Biomüll (m)	organic waste
bleifrei	lead free
Brennstoff (m)	fuel
chemisch	chemical
Energie (f)	energy
entsorgen	to dispose of
Fahrrad (n)	bicycle
Fahrradweg (m)	cycle path
filtern	to filter
Gebrauch (m)	usage
Gefahr (f)	danger
gefährlich	dangerous
heizen	to heat
Heizung (f)	heating
Insektizid (n)	insecticide
Kaugummi (m)	chewing gum
Kleidung (f)	clothes
Kohle (f)	coal
Kunststoff (m)	plastic
Lärm (m)	noise
laut	loud
Luft (f)	air

Luftverschmutzung (f)	air pollution
Müll (m)	rubbish
Mülltonne (f)	dustbin
öffentlich	public
Öltanker (m)	oil tanker
organisch	organic
Ozonloch (n)	ozone hole
Ozonschicht (f)	ozone layer
Pappe (f)	cardboard
Pestizid (n)	pesticide
Pfand (n)	deposit
produzieren	to produce
recyceln	to recycle
reinigen	to clean
sauber	clean
Sauerstoff (m)	oxygen
saurer Regen	acid rain
schaden	to damage
Schaden (m)	damage
schädlich	harmful
Schale (f)	shell
schmutzig	dirty
schützen	to protect
sparen	to save
Spraydose (f)	spray can
Treibhauseffekt (m)	greenhouse effect
Treibhausgas (n)	greenhouse gas
Trinkwasser (n)	drinking water
überbevölkert	overpopulated
ultraviolette Strahlen (pl)	ultraviolet rays
Umwelt (f)	environment
umweltfeindlich	eco-unfriendly

umweltfreundlich	eco-friendly
Verbrauch (m)	use
Verkehr (m)	traffic
Verkehrsmittel (n)	transport mode
Verpackung (f)	packaging
verschmutzen	to pollute
Verschmutzung (f)	pollution
verschwinden	to disappear
wegwerfen	to throw away
weltweit	worldwide
zerstören	to destroy
zu Fuß	on foot

Abholzung (f)	deforestation
Auspuffgase (pl)	car emissions
Düngemittel (n)	fertiliser
Einwegflasche (f)	disposable bottle
Hauptverkehrszeit (f)	rush hour
Kraftwerk (n)	power plant
Müllentsorgung (f)	waste disposal
Sprühdose (f)	spray can
überschreiten	to exceed
verpesten	to pollute
verwenden	to use
verschwenden	to waste
Verfallsdatum (n)	expiry date
wiederverwerten	to reuse

Auto (n) Zug (m) Boot (n) Bus (m) Fahrrad (n)

Flugzeug (n) Lastwagen (m) Mofa (n) Motorrad (n) Straßenbahn (f)

Now try this

Look at the forms of transport above. Write a sentence for each one, using the present tense for some and the past or future tense for others.

⑤ Work and education

School, college and future career

Abitur (n)	A levels
Abschlussprüfung (f)	final exam
AG (f)	school club
anfangen	to begin
Anspitzer (m)	sharpener
Antwort (f)	answer
antworten	to answer
Aufgabe (f)	exercise
Aula (f)	school hall
ausfüllen	to fill out
ausreichend	adequate
Austausch (m)	exchange
beantworten	to answer
befriedigend	satisfactory
beginnen	to begin
bekommen	to receive
Berufsberater (m)	careers advisor
Berufsschule (f)	vocational college
beschreiben	to describe
bestehen	to pass
Bibliothek (f)	library
Biologie (f)	biology
Bleistift (m)	pencil
Chemie (f)	chemistry
Chor (m)	choir
Deutsch	German
Direktor (m)	headmaster
durchfallen	to fail
enden	to end
Englisch	English
Erdkunde (f)	geography
Erfolg (m)	success
erfolgreich	successful
Fach (n)	subject
faul	lazy
Federmappe (f)	pencil case
Ferien (pl)	holidays
Filzstift (m)	felt pen
fleißig	hard-working
Frage (f)	question

fragen	to ask
Französisch	French
Fremdsprachen (pl)	languages
Füller (m)	fountain pen
Gang (m)	corridor
Gesamtschule (f)	secondary school
Geschichte (f)	history
Grundschule (f)	primary school
Gymnasium (n)	grammar school
Halle (f)	hall
Hauptschule (f)	secondary school
Hausaufgaben (pl)	homework
Hausmeister (m)	caretaker
Heft (n)	exercise book
Informatik (f)	ICT
Italienisch	Italian
Kantine (f)	canteen
Kindergarten (m)	nursery school
Klassenfahrt (f)	class trip
Klassenzimmer (n)	classroom
Klebstoff (m)	glue
klug	clever
Kochen (n)	cookery
kopieren	to copy
korrigieren	to correct
Kreide (f)	chalk
Kuli (m)	biro
Kunst (f)	art
Labor (n)	laboratory
Latein	Latin
Lehrer (m)	teacher
Lehrerzimmer (n)	staffroom
Leistung (f)	achievement
lernen	to learn
Lineal (n)	ruler
mangelhaft	poor
Mannschaft (f)	team
Mathe(matik) (f)	maths
Mittagspause (f)	lunch break
Mofa (n)	moped
mündlich	oral
Musik (f)	music

Naturwissenschaften (pl)	science
Note (f)	mark
Oberstufe (f)	sixth form
Pause (f)	break
Physik (f)	physics
Prüfung (f)	exam
Radiergummi (m)	rubber
Realschule (f)	secondary school
rechnen	to calculate
Religion (f)	RE
Resultat (n)	result
Schere (f)	scissors
schreiben	to write
schriftlich	written
Schulbuch (n)	textbook
Schule (f)	school
Schüler (m)	pupil
Schulhof (m)	playground
Schulleiter (m)	principal
Schultag (m)	schoolday
schwach	weak
schwer	difficult
Seite (f)	page, side
Sekretariat (n)	school office
Semester (n)	term ($\frac{1}{2}$ year)
sitzenbleiben	to repeat year
SMV (f)	school council
Spanisch	Spanish
Sporthalle (f)	sports hall
Sportplatz (m)	sports ground
Sprache (f)	language
staatlich	state
stark	strong
Stundenplan (m)	timetable
Tafel (f)	board
Taschenrechner (m)	calculator
Theatergruppe (f)	drama group
Turnen (n)	gymnastics
üben	to practise
Übung (f)	exercise
ungenügend	unsatisfactory
(un)gerecht, (un)fair	unfair

Mathe(matik) (f) Biologie (f) Chemie (f) Physik (f) Deutsch

Englisch Französisch Spanisch Erdkunde (f) Geschichte (f) Religion (f) Informatik (f) Kunst (f) Sport (m)

Now try this

What GCSEs are you and your friends taking? Check that you can say and write all the subjects in German. If you're thinking of taking A levels, can you name those subjects too?

5 Work and education

Unterricht (m)	lesson
unterrichten	to teach
Versammlung (f)	assembly
verstehen	to understand
weitermachen	to continue
Werken (n)	DT
wiederholen	to repeat
Wörterbuch (n)	dictionary
zeichnen	to draw
Zeichnen (n)	drawing
Zettel (m)	note
Zeugnis (n)	report
zuhören	to listen
zumachen	to close

abschreiben	to copy
abwesend	absent
Ausbildungsplatz (m)	apprenticeship
Aussprache (f)	pronunciation
aussprechen	to pronounce
Besprechung (f)	meeting
Bewerber (m)	applicant
Bindestrich (m)	hyphen
„blau" machen	to skive
eine Frage stellen	to ask a question
Entfernung (f)	distance
Ergebnis (n)	result
erklären	to explain
Fachhochschule (f)	college
Ganztagsschule (f)	all-day school
Internat (n)	boarding school
Klassenarbeit (f)	class test
Kugelschreiber (m)	biro
Mittlere Reife (f)	GCSE equivalent
nachsitzen	to have detention
notwendig	necessary
Pflichtfach (n)	core subject
Sozialkunde (f)	PSHCE
Strafarbeit (f)	lines
Studienplatz (m)	college place
vereinbaren	to agree
versetzt werden	to be moved
Wahlfach (n)	optional subject

Wirtschaftslehre (f)	economics
Abschlussprüfung (f)	final exam

Current and future jobs

Angestellte (m/f)	employee
anrufen	to phone
Anzeige (f)	advert
Apotheker (m)	chemist
Arbeit (f)	work
arbeiten	to work
Arbeiter (m)	worker
Arbeitgeber (m)	employer
Arbeitserfahrung (f)	work experience
Arbeitspraktikum (n)	work experience
Ausbildung (f)	education
Bäcker (m)	baker
Bauarbeiter (m)	builder
bauen	to build
Bauer (m)	farmer
Beamte (m)	civil servant
Bedingung (f)	condition
Begeisterung (f)	enthusiasm
beiliegend	attached
bereit	prepared
Beruf (m)	job
berufstätig	employed
beschäftigt	busy
beschließen	to decide
besitzen	to own
Besitzer (m)	owner
Betrieb (m)	company
bewerben (sich um)	to apply (for)
Bewerbung (f)	application
Bezahlung (f)	pay
Brief (m)	letter
Briefkasten (m)	letter box
Briefmarke (f)	stamp
Briefträger (m)	postman
Briefumschlag (m)	envelope
Büro (n)	office
Chef (m)	boss
Ehrlichkeit (f)	honesty
einstellen	to appoint
Elektriker (m)	electrician

empfehlen	to recommend
entscheiden (sich)	to decide
Erfahrung (f)	experience
erklären	to explain
Fahrer (m)	driver
fertig	ready
Feuerwehrmann (m)	fireman
Firma (f)	firm
Firmenchef (m)	company boss
Fleischer (m)	butcher
ganztags	full-time
Ganztagsjob (m)	full-time job
garantieren	to guarantee
Gehalt (n)	salary
Gelegenheit (f)	opportunity
Handy (n)	mobile phone
Hausfrau (f)	housewife
Hausmann (m)	house husband
im Freien	outdoors
Ingenieur (m)	engineer
jobben	to temp
Kandidat (m)	candidate
Karriere (f)	career
Kassierer (m)	cashier
Kauffrau (f)	business-woman
Kaufmann (m)	businessman
Kellner (m)	waiter
Klempner (m)	plumber
Koch (m)	cook
Kollege (m)	colleague
Kontakt (m)	contact
kündigen	to resign
Kündigung (f)	resignation
Lebenslauf (m)	CV
LKW-Fahrer (m)	lorry driver
Lohn (m)	wages
Maler (m)	painter
Mechaniker (m)	mechanic
Messe (f)	trade fair
Metzger (m)	butcher
mitteilen	to inform
möglich	possible
müssen	to have to
Nachricht (f)	message
Nebenjob (m)	part-time job
organisieren	to organise
Pfarrer (m)	vicar
plaudern	to chat
Polizei (f)	police
Postbote (m)	postman
Postkarte (f)	postcard

Now try this

Write out all the verbs on this page in German. Close the book and try to write the English for each one. Check back, then write out again any that you did not know.

⑤ Work and education

Priester (m)	priest	Tierarzt (m)	vet	Fußgängerüberweg (m)	pedestrian bridge
Punkt (m)	point	Tischler (m)	joiner	Gebiet (n)	area
Qualifikation (f)	qualification	verdienen	to earn	Gelegenheitsarbeit (f)	casual labour
Schauspieler (m)	actor	Verkäufer (m)	salesman		
Schichtarbeit (f)	shift work	versuchen	to try	Gesetz (n)	law
schicken	to send	von zu Hause arbeiten	to work from home	Gleitzeit (f)	flexitime
Schrägstrich (m)	slash			hitzefrei	day off (too hot)
Schulbildung (f)	education	Werkstatt (f)	studio, workshop		
Sekretärin (f)	secretary			Landwirt (m)	farmer
selbstständig	independent	Ziel (n)	goal	lehren	to teach
senden	to send	zurückrufen	to phone back	Rechtsanwalt (m)	lawyer
sitzen	to sit			Schichtarbeit (f)	shiftwork
Sorge (f)	worry			Schriftsteller (m)	author
Stadtführer (m)	city guide			Schulhalbjahr (n)	school term
stehen	to stand			sicherlich	certainly
Stelle (f)	position	absagen	to cancel	Unternehmen (n)	company
Streik (m)	strike	Anstreicher (m)	painter	Unterstrich (m)	underline
Teilnahme (f)	participation	anwesend sein	to be present	verbinden	to connect
Teilzeitarbeit (f)	part-time work	ausfallen	to be cancelled	vereinbaren	to agree
		Bewerber (m)	applicant	Vorstellungs- gespräch (n)	job interview
Teilzeitjob (m)	part-time job	Besprechung (f)	meeting		
Telefon (n)	telephone	Dolmetscher (m)	interpreter		
Telefonbuch (n)	telephone book	Einzelhändler (m)	retailer		
		entschließen (sich)	to decide		
telefonieren	to telephone				
Tellerwäscher (m)	pot-washer	Fließband (n)	assembly line		
Termin (m)	appointment	Flohmarkt (m)	flea market		

der Arzt   die Ärztin

die Krankenschwester
der Krankenpfleger

der Friseur   die Friseuse

der Polizist   die Polizistin

die Gärtnerin   der Gärtner

die Zahnärztin   der Zahnarzt

Now try this

To help you learn the jobs vocabulary, make a list of five jobs that you would like to do and five jobs that you would not like to do and then memorise them.

Answers

Lifestyle

1. Birthdays
1 B – 30th October
2 D – 17th May
3 A – 29th March

2. Pets
B – She would love to have a dog.
C – Her home is unsuitable.

3. Physical description
(a) The suspect was 17 years old. T
(b) He wasn't wearing any jewellery. F
(c) His dog was not on a lead. ?
(d) The suspect has been caught. T

4. Character description
A – Dominant, B – Funny,
D – Adventurous,
F – Sometimes cross

5. Brothers and sisters
(a) Her parents separated.
(b) She can't stand him.

10. Eating at home
(a) Chicken: L
(b) Vegetables: L + S
(c) Soup: S

11. Eating in a café
1 Llayda: A – mineral water
2 Lukas: C – ice-cream
3 Benjamin: C – kebab

12. Eating in a restaurant
1 (a) It was worth the cost.
  (b) So she can go back to the restaurant.
2 (a) It was chaotic. / There was a really long queue.
  (b) He felt sorry for the staff (having to work so hard).

13. Healthy eating
B – Frannie is keen to have a healthy diet.
C – Frannie's mother cares about what Frannie eats.

15. Health problems
(a) I have health issues: L + S
(b) Cigarettes have a negative effect on my sports performance: L
(c) I think cigarettes damage your health: L + S
(d) I suffer from a cough: S

17. Social issues
Racism must be eradicated

18. Social problems
C – He thinks his group may have a solution.

Leisure

19. General hobbies
1 B – Television
2 A – Music
3 C – Reading

21. Arranging to go out
1 Vincenz: D – I would prefer to stay at home.
2 Tatjana: E – I need new shoes.
3 Patrik: A – I am going to a wedding.

22. What I did last weekend
(a) Her boyfriend's 18th birthday.
(b) Watched videos of him as a child.
(c) Go for a walk in the woods.
(d) To finish her book as it was so exciting.

23. TV programmes
Positive: She finds cartoons funny.
Negative: You have to pay to watch some sport programmes and pay too much for the latest films.

25. Music
Max: E – clarinet
Pia-Maria: A – guitar
Martin: D – drums

26. New technology
A – Mia is nosey.
C – Mia is not worried by her parents' threats.
D – Mia needs the computer for schoolwork.

27. Language of the internet
(a) So he could get in touch with other people who shared his interests.
(b) He had found like-minded people.

29. Shops
F – Music shop, E – Electrical shop, A – Florist's (any order)

30. Food shopping
B – She was surprised by the cost of the honey.

32. Clothes and colours
1 Daniela: C – jacket
2 Leona: A – skirt
3 Ida: D – jumper

34. Returning clothes
1 C – She hasn't got her receipt.
2 B – She has a job interview tomorrow.

35. Shopping opinions
(a) N
(b) P

36. Pocket money
1 Kristin: C – My attitude to pocket money has changed.
2 Silas: E – I would like to have more control over my spending.
3 Sandra: B – In return for pocket money I have to do jobs at home.

39. Booking accommodation
B – Two rooms on the same floor and parking

40. Staying in a hotel
H – lag, E – Hallenbad,
A – Familienzimmer, F – sehen,
J – reservieren, G – Nachteile

41. Staying on a campsite
(a) She was afraid the course would be fully booked, as kayaking has become so popular (recently).
(b) Because she will need a shower after a long day on the water.
(c) Water fountains in each zone / area.
(d) There will always be fresh water right by the tent and she won't need to carry bottles / buckets to a central area to fetch water.

42. Holiday activities
B – Climbing, D – Theme parks (any order)

43. Holiday preferences
Kodra: B – I don't mind staying at home in the holidays.

Annika: C – We always go to the same place.

Matthias: B – I dread the Christmas holidays.

45. Past holidays
1 Kuschtrin: A – Swimming
2 Bierta: B – Climbing
3 Romeo: D – Skiing

Home and environment

47. My house
(a) A flat.
(b) There is a park nearby.

48. My room
Georg's room: C – Paint the walls.
Anna's room: B – Change her curtains.

50. Where I live
(a) B – werfen
(b) A – ruhiger

51. Places in town
(a) P – enjoys going to the cinema
(b) B – likes shopping
(c) S – is interested in buildings
(d) K – likes swimming
(e) S – goes to the old part of town

52. What to do in town
1 C – His friends
2 A – I don't enjoy the excursions with relatives.

54. Signs in town
1 No smoking – B
2 Pull the door – G
3 Dogs are welcome – C
4 Throw rubbish in the bin – E
5 Entrance on the left – F

56. Town description
1 Hamburg, North
2 Dresden, East
3 Munich, South
4 Kassel, central/middle

57. Weather
1 B – will lessen on Tuesday
2 A – be colder than the coast

58. Celebrations at home
1 Nina: P + N
2 Lars: P
3 Gabi: N

60. At the train station
1 Departure: 16.00; Arrival: 20.10
2 Departure: 12.03; Arrival 14.22
3 Departure: 19.30; Arrival: 21.15

62. Transport
(a) Better than in England.
(b) More investment in buses / trains.

63. The environment
(a) People's means of transport have changed. F
(b) Transporting fuel is expensive. ?
(c) Water pollution is no longer an issue. F
(d) You can donate money to help combat air pollution. ?

64. Environmental issues
(a) Too much plastic packaging used in shops.
(b) We travel too much by car
(c) Any two: Too much traffic./Get stuck in traffic jams./Air more polluted./Global warming.
(d) Travel by public transport./Go by bike./Go on foot if you have no bike.

65. What I do to be 'green'
A – It provides its own solar energy.
D – It is extremely environmentally friendly.

66. News headlines
1 C – Arbeitsplatz
2 B – Hungersnot

Work and education

67. School subjects
1 Negative (any one): Finds maths difficult. / Doesn't understand maths lessons. / Can't complete maths homework.
2 Positive (any one): Thinks history and geography are great / interesting. / Likes learning about other countries / people.

69. School routine
B – Beth does homework on the journey.
C – Beth has to be in class at ten past 8.

71. Primary school
1 A – ignored his father
2 C – in different ways

72. Rules at school
1 There is an exam on. – D
2 Teresa is looking for the school rules. – F
3 No chewing gum. – A
4 Keep your mobile phone in your bag. – E

73. School problems
1 D – Leistungsdruck
2 A – Abschlussprüfung
3 C – Direktor
4 F – bewältigen

75. Future careers
A – He has an annoying boss.
D – It is a big company.

76. Jobs
1 (a) Sales assistant
  (b) Saturdays 9 till 12
2 (a) Any two: She is a nurse. / She works long hours. / She has an exhausting job.
  (b) Any two: He works in IT. / He works from home. / He finds his work interesting.

77. Job adverts
1 Sonia: E
2 Peter: A
3 Karola: D

79. Job application
(a) Nancy finds skiing tiring. ?
(b) Nancy can speak three languages. T
(c) Nancy has never had a holiday job before. F
(d) Her experience of work has been positive and negative. T
(e) Nancy hopes to stay with a penfriend in England. F

81. Opinions about jobs
1 P + N
2 N
3 P
4 P
5 P + N

82. Part-time work
(a) Look for a part-time job.
(b) Stacking the shelves in a supermarket / working in a local café.
(c) They have to be 18 years old.
(d) It is a first step on the way to independence.

84. My work experience
B – His colleagues were too busy to help him.

Grammar

85. Gender and plurals
(a) die Anmeldung / die Anmeldungen
(b) der Fahrer / die Fahrer
(c) das Rührei / die Rühreier
(d) die Haltestelle / die Haltestellen
(e) der Fernseher / die Fernseher
(f) das Brötchen / die Brötchen

86. Cases 1
(a) gegen die Mauer
(b) außer einem Kind
(c) trotz des Schnees
(d) nach einer Stunde
(e) zu den Geschäften
(f) ohne ein Wort
(g) während des Sommers
(h) beim Arzt

87. Cases 2
(a) der   **(e)** der
(b) den   **(f)** den
(c) dem   **(g)** den
(d) die   **(h)** die

88. Cases 3
(a) I don't want to go shopping.
(b) She spent all her pocket money on clothes.
(c) Many people quickly become impolite.
(d) I find my life boring.
(e) This time we are going by train.
(f) His parents are unemployed.
(g) I find such rules stupid.
(h) Which book are you reading?

89. Adjective endings
(a) ausgezeichnete
(b) warmes
(c) preisgünstiges
(d) zentrale
(e) beliebte
(f) meistverkauften
(g) verkaufsoffenen
(h) persönlichen

90. Comparisons
(a) einfacher
(b) jünger
(c) besser
(d) nützlicher
(e) kleinste
(f) langweiligste
(g) beliebteste
(h) schlechtesten

91. Personal pronouns
(a) sie   **(d)** uns
(b) mir   **(e)** mir; ihm
(c) dir   **(f)** mir

92. Word order
Possible answers:
(a) Ich fahre gern ins Ausland.
(b) Man findet die Informationen beim Verkehrsamt.
(c) Normalerweise esse ich gesund.
(d) Manchmal sehen wir im Jugendklub Filme.
(e) Im Juli möchte ich im Sportzentrum arbeiten.
(f) Letztes Jahr habe ich in einem Büro gearbeitet.
(g) Morgen gehe ich mit meiner Mutter ins Kino.

93. Conjunctions

(a) Ich habe bei meiner Großmutter gewohnt, während meine Mutter im Krankenhaus war.

(b) Ich bin ins Café gegangen, nachdem ich ein T-Shirt gekauft habe.

(c) Ich war in Spanien im Urlaub, als ich einen neuen Freund kennengelernt habe.

(d) Er ist sehr beliebt, obwohl er nicht sehr freundlich ist.

(e) Wenn ich einen Nebenjob finde, werde ich auf eine neue Gitarre sparen.

(f) Ich bin froh, dass ich in der Schule gute Noten bekommen habe.

(g) Ich muss meine Eltern fragen, ob ich ins Konzert gehen darf.

94. More on word order

1 (a) Ich fahre nach Italien, um meine Verwandten zu besuchen.

(b) Ich gehe zum Sportzentrum, um 5 Kilo abzunehmen.

2 (a) Ich versuche, anderen zu helfen.

(b) Ich habe vor, auf die Uni zu gehen.

3 (a) Das ist das Geschäft, das Sommerschlussverkauf hat.

(b) Hier ist eine Kellnerin, die sehr unhöflich ist.

95. The present tense

(a) höre

(b) schläft

(c) geht

(d) Isst

(e) fahren

(f) machen

(g) Gibt

(h) bleibt

96. More on verbs

1 (a) Ich sehe fern. Ich habe ferngesehen.

(b) Ich steige um sechs Uhr um. Ich bin um sechs Uhr umgestiegen.

(c) Ich lade Musik herunter. Ich werde Musik herunterladen.

(d) Ich habe abgewaschen. Ich muss abwaschen.

2 (a) mich

(b) uns

(c) euch

(d) dich

97. Commands

To pay attention to their darlings and not to use the green spaces and paths as a dog toilet.

98. Present tense modals

(a) Ich muss um einundzwanzig Uhr ins Bett gehen.

(b) In der Schule darf man nicht rauchen.

(c) Du sollst den Tisch decken!

(d) Kannst du mir zu Hause helfen?

(e) Ich will in den Ferien Ski fahren.

(f) Ich möchte am Wochenende fernsehen.

(g) Meine Freunde müssen mit dem Bus fahren.

(h) Ich kann das Problem nicht lösen.

99. Imperfect modals

1 (a) Ich musste Hausaufgaben machen.

(b) Sie konnten mir nicht helfen.

(c) Er wollte eine neue Hose kaufen.

(d) Wir sollten das Zimmer aufräumen.

(e) In der Schule durfte man nie Kaugummi kauen.

(f) Alle Schüler mussten bis sechzehn Uhr bleiben.

2 (a) Es könnte schwierig werden.

(b) Ich möchte nach Berlin fahren.

100. The perfect tense 1

(a) Ich habe eine Jacke gekauft.

(b) Wir sind nach Portugal geflogen.

(c) Ich habe meinen Freund gesehen.

(d) Lena und Hannah sind in die Stadt gegangen.

(e) Ich habe meine Tante besucht.

(f) Ich bin im Hotel geblieben.

(g) Was hast du zu Mittag gegessen?

(h) Am Samstag hat er Musik gehört.

101. The perfect tense 2

(a) Ich habe zu viele Kekse gegessen.

(b) Haben Sie gut geschlafen?

(c) Wir haben uns am Bahnhof getroffen.

(d) Ich war krank, weil ich den ganzen Tag gestanden habe.

(e) Ich weiß, dass du umgestiegen bist.

(f) Warum hast du die E-Mail geschrieben?

(g) Ich habe ihr empfohlen, dass sie nicht mitkommen sollte.

(h) Ich war sehr traurig, als er gestorben ist.

Answers

102. The imperfect tense
(a) She was scared.
(b) It was hopeless.
(c) Where was it hurting?
(d) Did you hear that?
(e) Suddenly the man came towards us.
(f) That was a surprise, wasn't it?
(g) There was no one at home.
(h) They enjoyed playing table tennis.

103. The future tense
(a) Ich werde das Spiel gewinnen.
(b) Wir werden in den Freizeitpark gehen.
(c) Sie werden eine große Wohnung mieten.
(d) Ihr werdet große Schwierigkeiten haben.
(e) Er wird die Prüfung bestehen.
(f) Nächste Woche werden wir umziehen.
(g) Wirst du dich heute schminken?
(h) Ich werde mich um sechs Uhr anziehen.

104. The conditional
(a) Ich würde gern ins Theater gehen.
(b) Er würde nie zu spät ankommen.
(c) Wir würden nie Drogen nehmen.
(d) Würden Sie mir bitte helfen?
(e) Zum Geburtstag würde sie am liebsten Geld bekommen.
(f) Nächstes Jahr würden sie vielleicht heiraten.
(g) Wenn Latein Pflicht wäre, würde ich auf eine andere Schule gehen.
(h) Wenn ich das machen würde, würde es Krach mit meinen Eltern geben.

105. The pluperfect tense
(a) Ich hatte zu Mittag gegessen.
(b) Sie hatten als Stadtführer gearbeitet.
(c) Warst du schwimmen gegangen?
(d) Wir waren in Kontakt geblieben.
(e) Sie waren mit dem Rad in die Stadt gefahren.
(f) Ich hatte sie vor einigen Monaten besucht, aber damals war sie schon krank.
(g) Bevor ich ins Haus gegangen war, hatte ich ein Gesicht am Fenster gesehen.
(h) Obwohl ich kaum mit ihm gesprochen hatte, schien er sehr freundlich zu sein.

106. Questions
1 (a) Lesen Sie gern Science-Fiction-Bücher?
  (b) Finden Sie Ihre Arbeit anstrengend?
  (c) Möchten Sie nur Teilzeit arbeiten?
  (d) Werden Sie nächsten Sommer nach Australien auswandern?
2 (a) Wer ist/Wie heißt Ihr Lieblingssänger?
  (b) Wann sind Sie das letzte Mal ins Theater gegangen?
  (c) Warum sind Sie Lehrer(in) geworden?
  (d) Wie oft essen Sie im Restaurant?
  (e) Was für Geschäfte mögen Sie besonders?

107. Time markers
(a) Seit drei Jahren spiele ich Klavier.
(b) Letzte Woche hat er die Hausaufgaben nicht gemacht.
(c) Nächsten Sommer werden wir in den Bergen wandern gehen.
(d) Am Anfang wollten wir das Betriebspraktikum nicht machen.
(e) In Zukunft wird man alle Lebensmittel elektronisch kaufen.
(f) Ich hoffe, eines Tages Disneyland zu besuchen.
(g) Vorgestern hatte ich Halsschmerzen.
(h) Früher haben sie oft Tennis gespielt.

108. Numbers
(a) 14.–23. Mai
(b) 07:45
(c) €3,80
(d) 27. Januar 1756
(e) €185 Millionen
(f) 15% Ermäßigung
(g) 16:35 Uhr
(h) 35 Grad

Your own notes

Published by Pearson Education Limited, Edinburgh Gate, Harlow, Essex, CM20 2JE.

www.pearsonschoolsandfecolleges.co.uk

Text © Pearson Education Limited 2013
Audio recorded at Tom Dick + Debbie Productions, © Pearson Education Limited
MFL Series Editor: Julie Green
Edited by Frances Reynolds and Sue Chapple
Typeset by Kamae Design, Oxford
Original illustrations © Pearson Education Limited 2013
Illustrations by KJA Artists and John Hallett
Cover illustration by Miriam Sturdee
Picture research by Kath Kollberg

The right of Harriette Lanzer to be identified as author of this work has been asserted by her in
accordance with the Copyright, Designs and Patents Act 1988.

First published 2013

16 15 14 13
10 9 8 7 6 5 4 3 2 1

British Library Cataloguing in Publication Data
A catalogue record for this book is available from the British Library

ISBN 978 1 447 94110 1

Printed in Slovakia by Neografia

Acknowledgements
The publisher would like to thank the following for their kind permission to reproduce their
photographs:

(Key: b-bottom; c-centre; l-left; r-right; t-top)
Alamy Images: Blickwinkel 55c, Catchlight Visual Services 49, David Crausby 61r, PE Forsberg
62, Imagebroker 55b, Michael Klinec 65, Jason Langley 17, Photos 12 24; Corbis: Lawrence
Manning 22; Getty Images: Bongarts 18, Alexander Walter 27; Pearson Education Ltd: Sophie
Bluy 35, 43, 69, 70, 83t, 83b, 104, 104r, MindStudio 77, Jules Selmes 55t; Rex Features: Sipa
Press 51; Shutterstock.com: Alexander Kalina 34, Alexander Raths 107, Andre Blais 95, Imants
O. 61l, Joshua Haviv 44, Maksym Gorpenyuk 38, Martin Valigursky 37, Masson 4, nakamasa 67,
.shock 20, Stephen Mcsweeny 34tr, Ulrich Willmünder 28, YanLev 40, Yuri Arcurs 98; The Kobal
Collection: Walt Disney / Vaughen, Stephen 100; Veer/Corbis: Galina Barskaya 41, erierika 58, Jill
66, Franz Pfluegl 21, sorymur 16; www.imagesource.com: 42

All other images © Pearson Education Limited

Every effort has been made to contact copyright holders of material reproduced in this book.
Any omissions will be rectified in subsequent printings if notice is given to the publishers.

In the writing of this book, no AQA examiners authored sections relevant to examination papers
for which they have responsibility.